William J. Fay

P9-DBT-352

PLEASURES
FOREVERMORE

PLEASURES
FOREVERMORE

THE THEOLOGY OF C. S. LEWIS

JOHN RANDOLPH WILLIS

A Campion Book

LOYOLA UNIVERSITY PRESS
CHICAGO

© 1983 John Randolph Willis, S.J.
Printed in the United States of America

ISBN 0-8294-0446-5

Acknowledgments

Grateful acknowledgment is given to the following publishers for permission to quote from their works.

WILLIAM COLLINS SONS & CO LTD

The Pilgrim's Regress, by C. S. Lewis. Copyright © 1933, 1943 by Clive Staples Lewis and now held by the estate of C. S. Lewis.

HARCOURT BRACE JOVANOVICH, INC

Letters to Malcolm: Chiefly on Prayer, by C. S. Lewis. Copyright © 1963, 1964 by the estate of C. S. Lewis and/or C. S. Lewis.
Letters of C. S. Lewis, edited by W. H. Lewis. Copyright © 1966 by W. H. Lewis and Executors of C. S. Lewis.

MACMILLAN PUBLISHING COMPANY, INC

The Magician's Nephew, by C. S. Lewis. Copyright © 1955 by C. S. Lewis.
Mere Christianity, by C. S. Lewis. Copyright © 1943, 1945, 1952 by Macmillan Publishing Co., Inc. Copyrights renewed.
The Problem of Pain, by C. S. Lewis. (New York: Macmillan, 1943).
The Silver Chair, by C. S. Lewis. Copyright © 1953 by the Trustees of the Estate of C. S. Lewis, renewed 1981 y Arthur Owen Barfield.
The Screwtape Letters, Copyright © 1942 by C. S. Lewis.

For Harvey and the
Jesuit Community at Boston College

At thy right hand there are pleasures forevermore.

Psalm 16:11

Table of Contents

Foreword

It is a cause of much joy to me that this is the first book about C. S. Lewis to be written by a Roman Catholic priest. And if that wasn't enough, one by such a congenial priest as Father Willis. Indeed, it is because I like the author so much that I believe he will not be offended that I take exception to a double claim found in his Introduction. The first is that Lewis's *Mere Christianity* represents "the via media of the Anglican church." The second is that "Lewis's foundations for *Mere Christianity* must collapse, because the very topics which he attempted to avoid—Pope, magisterium, sacraments—are essential ingredients to the theological whole."

What is true is that the Anglican Church is most unfortunate in not having a seat of doctrinal Authority. That has always weighed against it, and this is as responsible as anything for the recent divisions caused, in some places, by the creation of priestesses. Even so, it *does* believe in the Sacraments. All seven of them —Baptism, Confirmation, Mass, Penance, Matrimony, Orders, and Extreme Unction. In fact, it is because the Anglican Church has preserved the Sacraments that His Holiness Pope John Paul II and the Archbishop of Canterbury have reason to hope for a reunion of these two communions of the Apostolic Church. I don't know of anyone who wanted that unity so much as C. S. Lewis. But unity has to be "about" something and it is that very big "Something" which Lewis worked so hard to get people to understand.

Because of Lewis's enormous contribution as an apologist of the Faith—of which this book is ample testimony—it is generally unknown that *he* called himself a "medievalist." This is because he was the Fellow of English Language and Literature at Magdalen College, Oxford, from 1925 through 1953, and the Professor of Medieval and Renaissance English Literature in the University of Cambridge from 1954 until his death in 1963. I have found, through twenty years correspondence with his admirers, that his "official" job causes as much of a surprise for some as does the discovery that the author of *Alice in Wonderland* spent his working life as a teacher of mathematics in Oxford. But all of this Father Willis deals with in his first chapter. Even so, I would like to draw attention to the first paragraph of Lewis's *Preface to "Paradise Lost,"* as it contains much that every writer and critic would do well to consider. "The first qualification," said Lewis

> for judging any piece of workmanship from a corkscrew to a cathedral is to know *what* it is—what it was intended to do and how it is meant to be used. After that has been discovered the temperance reformer may decide that the corkscrew was made for a bad purpose, and the communist may think the same about the cathedral. But such questions come later. The first thing is to understand the object before you: as long as you think the corkscrew was meant for opening tins or the cathedral for entertaining tourists you can say nothing to the purpose about them.

Now, most of us are so used to book reviewers talking about nearly everything under the sun that we sometimes have to glance at the top of the page to discover the name of the book under review. If it happens to be a book we specially care for, this practice makes us peevish. If it's a book we have already read, one perhaps written by a friend, we become more peevish still. "Can't this reviewer," we ask, "tell a corkscrew from a cathedral?"

But the immediate question is "What has all this to do with C. S. Lewis?" The answer is—quite a lot. Although his readers don't appear to notice any "change of voice" in his books, some—such as the Narnian Chronicles—were written simply because he enjoyed it. A few were written at the request of others, and *Mere Christianity* is one of those. In fact, it didn't originate in his mind as a book at all. What happened was that the British Broadcasting Corporation asked him to give a series of four fifteen-minute talks over the radio. The impact of those talks was so great that the B.B.C. asked for another series, and another, until in the end—well, there was *Mere Christianity*. However, from the beginning there was a lot of talk going on behind the scenes. It was mainly about how, in such short radio talks, Lewis could—as was the intention of the B.B.C.—reach the "Great British Public." A "public" made up—as it is in the United States—of Christians of all the denominations and most people who aren't Christians at all. Because of this, Lewis knew that his only chance of helping anyone was to confine his broadcasts to those elements which all Christians believe. Most people had never heard anything like it, and they were entranced. "Entranced" because, odd as it may seem, there had hitherto been few broadcasts and few books about those elements in Christianity which unite us, but a great many about those things which (however true and important) divide us.

It is not at all unreasonable that Father Willis should wish that Lewis had said more about the visible Church. I do too. But not if it wrecked the possibility of Lewis telling a mainly unbelieving world what Christianity is about. Or if it built even higher partitions between those who do believe. As it was, Lewis received letters from some who thought he should be burnt at the stake for mentioning the Virgin Birth. But to return to the "corkscrew or cathedral" intention behind *Mere Christianity*, that is very clearly defined in Lewis's preface to that book. I quote part of it here because it really is an intention which was followed in most of Lewis's books on religion. He said:

> Ever since I became a Christian I have thought that the best, perhaps the only, service I could do for my unbelieving neighbours was to explain and defend the belief that has been common to nearly all Christians at all times. I had more than one reason for thinking this. In the first place, the questions which divide Christians from one another often involve points of high Theology or even of ecclesiastical history which ought never to be treated except by real experts. I should have been out of my depth in such waters: more in need of help myself than able to help others. And secondly, I think we must admit that the discussion of these disputed points has no tendency at all to bring an outsider into the Christian fold. So long as we write and talk about them we are much more likely to deter him from any Christian communion than to draw him into our own. Our divisions should never be discussed except in the presence of those who have already come to believe that there is one God and that Jesus Christ is His only Son.

At this point I hope I will not be thought presumptuous if I asked the reader a question. Suppose you were entertaining in your home some people whom you liked but who had never been exposed to the Christian faith. Suppose, further, that you desire with all your heart to see them converted. What would happen if, just as they sat down to eat, you began to explain the doctrine of Infallibility? I believe, and you believe, it to be not only true but of very great importance. But is that the place to *begin?*

It is interesting to me—and I'm certain it will be to my friend Father Willis—that *Mere Christianity* made a favourable impression on many of the Jesuits of Campion Hall, Oxford. So much so that they asked Lewis to talk to them about Christian reunion. I think this must have been shortly after Lewis had completed his *Mere Christianity* broadcasts, as the fragment which survives of this talk is written on the back of one of his broadcast scripts.

After deploring the lack of agreement between Anglicans and Roman Catholics, he went on to say:

> I know no way of bridging this gulf. Nor do I think it the business of the private layman to offer much advice on bridge-building to his betters. My only function as a Christian writer is to preach "mere Christianity" not *ad clerum* but *ad populum*. Any success that has been given me has, I believe, been due to my strict observance of those limits. By attempting to do otherwise I should only add one more recruit (and a very ill qualified recruit) to the ranks of the controversialists. After that I should be no more use to anyone . . .
>
> When we find a certain heavenly unity existing between really devout persons of differing creeds—a mutual understanding and even a power of mutual edification which each may lack towards a lukewarm member of his own denomination—we must ascribe this to the work of Christ who, in the erroneous one, sterilises his errors and inhibits the evil consequences they would naturally have ("If ye drink any deadly thing it shall not hurt you") and opens the eyes of the other party to all the truths mingled in his friend's errors, which are, of course, likely to be truths he particularly needs.

Being the devout Christian he was, Lewis went to Mass every Sunday and on all major feasts. He went to confession every Friday, for years at a monastery, and for a very long time at the twelfth-century church of St. Mary Magdalen in the heart of Oxford. It was from that church that, near the end of his life, he received Extreme Unction and it's there I say an annual Requiem Mass for his immortal soul. Given all this, can one really suppose that his constant reiterations of the great truths of the holy, Catholic and Apostolic Church came from one who had no belief in the visible Church? He did more good than we shall ever know. And much of that good resulted from the fact that he knew his limits. Near the end of his life I was living in his house as his private secretary. Lewis had been forced by ill health to occupy a downstairs room. As a result, I slept in the bedroom which had been his. Over my head there was a crucifix and on the opposite wall a picture of the Turin Shroud.

As far back as 1939 Lewis had said in a letter to his former pupil, Dom Bede Griffiths, "Nothing would give such strong support to the Papal claims as the spectacle of a Pope actually functioning as head of Christendom." Yes, yes. A thousand times— Yes. But for me, who could ever fill that great hole caused by the death of the man whose fun, wisdom, generosity and blazing charity had been half my world? Would there ever be anyone who even *reminded* me of Lewis? I thought not. But, thanks be to God, he has come like the crest of a thousand-foot wave in the form of Pope John Paul II.

Finally, I hope this book will give as much pleasure to others as it has to me. Certainly it has one of the most delightful "faults" a book could have. Despite Father Willis's immense erudition, he loves what he is doing so much that it's almost impossible to say where he leaves off and Lewis begins. Or is it the other way round?

Walter Hooper
Oxford

Preface

My first introduction to C. S. Lewis came during World War II through the celebrated *Screwtape Letters* and the shorter books which now comprise *Mere Christianity*. At the same time, I was deeply immersed in Robert Lowry Calhoun's History of Christian Thought course at Yale University. But it was not until much later that the thought was suggested to me by my good friend Father Harvey D. Egan, S.J. that an in-depth study of Lewis would be a fine way to conclude a series on the development of Christian thought. It was not long before I had read my way through the entire Lewis corpus.

In the summer of 1979 I visited Wheaton College in Wheaton, Illinois and made thorough use of the fine Marion E. Wade Collection, which was started by Prof. Clyde S. Kilby in 1965. My deepest thanks go to him and his fine secretarial staff for their never-failing and gracious help. Prof. Chad Walsh was one of the earliest admirers of C. S. Lewis, and I am indebted to him for his warm encouragement and magic words: "Why, you're ready to write!" The C. S. Lewis Society of New York allowed me to inflict a learned paper on them, and although they were not always in agreement with some of my interpretations, I was the recipient of a warm reception from many good friends like Gene McGovern,

Emilie and William Griffin, Hope Kirkpatrick, the able secretary of the Society, Michael Christensen and many, many others. Of inestimable value is the expertise of the Reverend Walter Hooper and the trustees of the C. S. Lewis estate. Father Hooper is the acknowledged expert sans pareil on C. S. Lewis, and his help has been indispensable.

I need also to be mindful of the good help of my Jesuit brothers, and especially Father James L. Monks, S.J. and Father Patrick J. Ryan, S.J. who read the manuscript and made many very valuable suggestions. At the Loyola University Press, Father Daniel L. Flaherty, S.J. and Father Frederick M. Henley, S.J. were constant sources of encouragement, and boundless praise goes to Ms. Deborah Astudillo for her superb editorial work and her many helpful comments and observations. Needless to say, any errors, omissions, and shortcomings are my own, for which I bear the entire responsibility.

Introduction

There is no doubt that C. S. Lewis is one of the most popular theologians being read today. Virtually everyone has read *The Screwtape Letters*, and *Mere Christianity* is not very far behind in popularity. What we have in Lewis is primarily an ecumenical venture; the aim of his Christian writings is to present the fundamentals of orthodox Christianity to his readers, avoiding as far as possible controversial issues. But he is nonetheless alarmed by a too liberal Christianity, which he sees as being unfaithful to the ancient faith. His re-presentation of traditional doctrine indicates a desire to focus once again on catholic (small c) Christianity, and reinterpret it to a world bogged down in skepticism and moral relativism. The content of his message is therefore almost never original; he does not intend it to be. What is highly original, however, is his style of writing, his clearness of expression, his lucidity of thought, his illustrations, metaphors, analogies and, most of all, his charming winsomeness. Lewis's writing frequently presses for a decision; it is polemical writing in the best sense.

Actually Lewis is at least two persons. A number of his writings reflect his specialty of medieval and renaissance literature, which he taught for many years at Oxford and later at Cambridge. With these literary works (e.g., *The Allegory of Love*, *The Discarded*

Image, English Literature in the Sixteenth Century, the literary essays) I am not concerned, except insofar as certain theological ideas surface from time to time. Those interested in this part of Lewis's work can do no better than to consult Chad Walsh's fine study, *The Literary Legacy of C. S. Lewis.*

What I have attempted to do is to evaluate Lewis's theology from an avowedly Roman Catholic position. Although he remained an Anglican for his entire life (and was, in fact, put off by repeated inquiries as to why he did not become a Roman Catholic), Lewis has an enormous following among Roman Catholic readers. Surprisingly enough, he is even more popular with evangelical and even fundamentalist Christians, although he himself would no doubt feel uncomfortable in these categories. Lewis was a "Churchman" and not a radical Protestant sectary; he had a high regard for the place of liturgy and the sacraments in the life of the Church, even though he said he detested organ music.

This writer is a great admirer of C. S. Lewis, and considers him perhaps his foremost mentor. It might come, then, as something of a surprise to discover that he criticizes Lewis on what may seem to be his strong point—the Church. And even more devastating is his attempt to show that the basis for *Mere Christianity*, the via media of the Anglican church, does not from the Roman Catholic vantage point exist at all. Hence, from the logical point of view, Lewis's foundations for *Mere Christianity* must collapse, because the very topics he attempted to avoid—pope, magisterium, sacraments—are essential ingredients to the theological whole.

In the final analysis, however, it is of no matter that Lewis can be weighed and found wanting on certain Christian topics. He can certainly still be read, revered, and followed as one of the major theologians of the twentieth century.

The Reluctant Convert

Clive Staples Lewis was born in Belfast, Ireland on 29 November 1898. His father was a solicitor, whose Welsh background asserted itself in a sentimental, passionate, and rhetorical way. His mother was the daughter of a clergyman, and earned a B.A. from Queen's College in Belfast. Her temperament was cheerful and serene—a direct contrast to her husband's. Lewis had one sibling, an older brother named Warren, with whom he was very close. In 1905, the family moved to a new and larger house—later named "Little Lea"—which to the young Lewis seemed more like a city than a home. "The New House," he writes in his autobiography *Surprised by Joy*, "is almost a major character in my story. I am a product of long corridors, empty sunlit rooms, upstairs indoor silences, attics explored in solitude, distant noises of gurgling cisterns and pipes, and the noise of wind under the tiles."[1]

It was also the place of endless books, and early in life he became an omniverous reader. He had a lively imagination and began making up his own stories even before he could write. His literary interests for a period were anthropomorphized animals and knights in armor. These were combined to create tales of mice and rabbits who rode out in full mail to slay cats. Eventually Lewis wrote a history of "Animal-Land," as he called it, complete with maps. His brother's interest was India, and they managed to tie it in geographically with Animal-Land, including a series of steamship routes. Lewis's drawings often accompany his early literary efforts, and they indicate a real ability.

The family was in the habit of taking a vacation at the ocean each year. "In the course of one holiday," Warren writes, "my brother made the momentous decision to change his name. Disliking 'Clive,' and feeling various baby-names to be beneath his dignity, he marched up to my mother, put a forefinger on his chest, and announced, 'He is Jacksie.' He stuck to this the next day and thereafter, refusing to answer to any other name; Jacksie it had to be, a name contracted to Jacks and then to Jack. So to his family and his intimate friends, he was Jack for life . . ."[2]

Before Lewis was ten years old, his mother died of cancer. This had the effect of drawing him closer to his brother, as they both drew away from their father. He says that all that was tranquil and reliable disappeared from his life—the old security was gone; the family was breaking up. Warren had already entered the Wynyard School at Watford, Hertfordshire, England, and Jack followed in the fall of 1908.

This first educational experience was rather a horrible one. Lewis referred to the school as a concentration camp and later adjudged the headmaster to be insane. Fortunately Jack and Warren earned a reprieve when the school collapsed in the summer of 1910. But both boys blamed their father for having exercised his usual poor judgment in sending them there. Lewis says he did hear the doctrines of Christianity preached at Wynyard by some who genuinely believed them, and he himself began to read his Bible, act according to conscience, and enter into religious discussions. So the school was not a total loss.[3]

In the fall of 1910, Lewis entered Campbell College—not far

from his home. He remained there for only half the term, however, leaving both because of illness and because his father did not like the school. The best thing that happened to him there, he says, was to become thoroughly acquainted with *Sohrab and Rustum*.[4]

January 1911 found him at Cherbourg House in Malvern, where his real education began. He also made his first real friends—and he ceased to be a Christian. He developed an interest in a sort of romantic Occultism, which inflamed his imagination far more than his very simple theology had. Also fighting against his faith was a certain pessimism that had grown in him toward the existing world. He viewed life as a series of unremitting struggles in an unfortunate universe. He laid down the burden (which is what it had become) of his religion with some relief. In May of 1912 a character named Pogo arrived at the school and initiated Lewis into worldly sophistication. Thus, at Malvern, he suffered a loss of faith, of virtue and of simplicity.

In an interesting chapter in *Surprised by Joy* entitled "Bloodery," Lewis discusses the social setup of Malvern with its boys who were leaders (bloods), those who were followers (fags and tarts) and those who fell into neither group. This leads to a discussion of homosexuality and pederasty, which Lewis found prevalent in the school. However, his brother Warren disagrees, saying that much that Lewis writes about this is overdrawn.[5]

In April 1914 Lewis made the acquaintance of Joseph Arthur Greeves (1895–1968), who was to become a lifelong friend and correspondent.[6] Together they revelled in "Northerness." Lewis had felt a sharp stab of joy a few years earlier when he discovered *Siegfried and the Twilight of the Gods*, with illustrations by Arthur Rackham. By the time he met Greeves, he had become intensely interested in Norse mythology, including the works of Richard Wagner, and in all things "Northern." The fact that Greeves shared this interest—that he felt the same joy—drew

Lewis to him, and a firm friendship was established. This is not to say that Lewis abandoned his interest in the Greco-Roman tradition; "Northerness" simply added another facet to his romantic imagination. And it helped to offset the unpleasantness of the time he spent at Malvern.

Malvern finally became sufficiently unpalatable for Lewis to implore his father to take him away; so in the fall of 1914, he arrived at Bookham to study with William T. Kirkpatrick, "the Great Knock." "He was over six feet tall," Lewis tells us, "very shabbily dressed (like a gardener, I thought), lean as a rake, and immensely muscular. His wrinkled face seemed to consist entirely of muscles, so far as it was visible; for he wore moustache and side whiskers with a clean-shaven chin like the Emperor Franz Joseph."[7] "Kirk" stimulated in his student logical thinking, disputation, a recognition of the importance of evidence, and a clearcut dialectic. Some boys would not have liked him, but to Lewis his teaching was red beef and strong beer. After being knocked down sufficiently, Lewis began to put on intellectual muscle, and in the end became a not contemptible sparring partner.

Lewis developed into a still more voracious reader and became fond of hiking. And while he was never interested in group sports, he remained an inveterate walker until the end of his life. Meanwhile, Warren had been called into active service in World War I, although Jack makes virtually no mention of the conflict. By the time he had finished with the "Great Knock" (whom he then rated as his greatest teacher), he was well grounded in Greek, Latin, French and Italian, and had a fair grip on German. His bête noire was mathematics, which he never did master sufficiently to meet Oxford standards.

In March of 1916 Lewis made the acquaintance of George MacDonald's *Phantastes*, a book which he says "baptized his imagination with holiness." MacDonald was an obscure Scottish writer of the nineteenth century; his *Phantastes* was first published in 1858. It is a highly imaginative work, and its importance to Lewis lies in the fact that it presented to him a Christianized romanticism that he had previously overlooked. While the book did not convert him either intellectually or morally, it did show him that romanticism and Christianity were by no means incompatible. MacDonald had effectively cut the ground from under Lewis's atheism. He also made him reexamine his whole notion of "Joy." Joy (Sehnsucht) is Lewis's term for that sweet sense of longing that can come over one suddenly and is a special delight.

In December 1916 Lewis journeyed to Oxford for the first time to sit for a classical scholarship and, although passed over by New College, was elected to an open scholarship by University College. Oxford delighted him (he reports that he never saw a more beautiful place) and he promptly fell in love with it. The enchantment, however, was marred by the prospect of military service. From January to March of 1917, Lewis returned to Kirkpatrick to study for Responsions (the entrance examination for Oxford University), but mathematics was his undoing and he failed the exam. In April he began his studies at Oxford, but was recruited into the army before the term was out. He never did pass Responsions, for after the war a benevolent decree exempted ex-servicemen from taking it!

Passing through the ordinary course of training, he was commissioned as a Second Lieutenant in the Somerset Light Infantry, the old XIIIth Foot. He arrived at the front line trenches on his nineteenth birthday (29 November 1917), saw most of his service in the villages before Arras—Fampoux and Monchy—and was wounded at Mt. Bernechon, near Lillers, in April 1918.[8]

While in the billets at Keble College, Oxford, Lewis met and eventually roomed with an Irishman, Edward Francis Courtenay ("Paddy") Moore. He also got to know Paddy's mother, Mrs.

Janie King Moore, and after Paddy was killed in the war, Lewis became a kind of second son to her. Apparently he had made some sort of agreement with Paddy to look after his mother, but he refused to ever discuss his relationship with Mrs. Moore. She seems to have been Lewis's exact opposite, a somewhat shallow but domineering person who thought nothing of interrupting his serious study time with frivolous requests and unnecessary chores. Lewis endured this for years (until her death in 1951) without complaint. Why he did is unquestionably one of the great mysteries of his life. Warren, for his part, disliked her intensely.

Lewis returned to Oxford—"demobbed"—in January 1919. Here he began to make many lasting friendships, chief of which was that with Owen Barfield, who acted as a sort of anti-ego. A few months later, in March of 1919, Lewis's *Spirits in Bondage* was accepted for publication. It is a small volume of lyric poems and its general theme is that "nature is wholly diabolical and malevolent, and that God, if He exists, is outside of and in opposition to the cosmic arrangements. . . ."[9] The book received a few scant notices.

In the spring of 1920, Lewis took a first in Mods, and in June of 1922 took a first in Greats at Oxford. Meanwhile he had met William Butler Yeats on 14 March 1921, when he was invited to the Yeats home. He was also seriously at work on his long narrative poem *Dymer*, which was not to be published until July 1926. At this particular time, he was deeply involved in poetry and considered this to be his proper literary medium.

In spite of brilliant academic achievements (he took a first in English in 1923 and won the Chancellor's Prize for an English essay), Lewis had difficulty in locating a permanent teaching position at Oxford. His father agreed to provide for him for three more years, but that became unnecessary when in October 1924 he secured a one year appointment replacing E. F. Carritt, the famous philosopher. The following year came the good news that "The President and Fellows of Magdalen College have elected to an official Fellowship in the College as Tutor in English Language and Literature, for five years as from next June 25 [1925], Mr. Clive Staples Lewis, M.A. (University College),"[10] and at Magdalen College he was to remain until 1954.

Douglas Gilbert and Clyde S. Kilby have beautifully caught the serenity of these years in their splendid pictorial study *C. S. Lewis: Images of His World*. Lewis had excellent living quarters above the celebrated deer park; he was within a few minutes of Addison's Walk and the River Cherwell, and on holidays enjoyed taking long hikes in the area. Many notable persons became close friends: J. R. R. Tolkien, Nevill Coghill, H. V. D. Dyson, A. C. Harwood and C. T. Onions, and before long there were regular meetings of the Inklings—a group of Oxford friends who gathered together for serious discussion and light-hearted frivolity.

During the 1920s (and likewise during his own twenties), Lewis gradually moved from atheism to Christianity. The process of his conversion is somewhat complicated and can only be drastically condensed here. There were several contributing factors: good friends at Oxford, such as Nevill Coghill, who were both Christians and able scholars; his correspondence with Arthur Greeves; his reading of the specifically Christian authors such as Jakob Boehme; and his study of Samuel Alexander's *Space, Time and Deity*. It was Alexander who pointed out the difference between subject and object, between thinking and a thought, between hope and the thing hoped for. This helped to clarify Lewis's notion of Joy, which he now discovered always pointed to something else— something that was seemingly beyond his reach. It was not the wave, but the wave's imprint on the sand. All Joys said in the last resort, "It is not I. I am only a reminder. Look! Look! What do I remind you of?"[11]

Two other writers were also influential: J. G. Frazer (*The Golden Bough*) and G. K. Chesterton (*The Everlasting Man*). Frazer caused Lewis to realize that primitive and pre-Christian religions often adumbrate Christian truths, and that the frequent theme of the Dying and Rising God might actually have come to pass in Christianity. And Chesterton interpreted the whole Christian outline of history in a form which seemed to make sense. Riding on the top of a bus going up Headington Hill one day, Lewis felt himself given a free choice. He could open the door or keep it shut. "Neither choice was presented as a duty; no threat or promise was attached to either, though I knew that to open the door or take off the corslet meant the incalculable."[12] And yet it seemed impossible not to make the self-surrender.

In *Surprised by Joy*, Lewis writes: "You must picture me alone in that room in Magdalen, night after night, feeling, whenever my mind lifted even for a second from my work, the steady, unrelenting approach of Him whom I so earnestly desired not to meet. That which I greatly feared had at last come upon me. In the Trinity Term of 1929 I gave in, and admitted that God was God, and knelt and prayed: perhaps, that night, the most dejected and reluctant convert in all England."[13] But it is important to note that this was a conversion to Theism, not to Christianity.

The final act in the conversion drama seems to have occurred during a trip to Whipsnade Zoo. Lewis began to attend church and chapel services, and before long he had come to grips with the truth of the Incarnation. The strong appeal of Christianity is that it is an historical religion. The final step came for Lewis when he was driven to Whipsnade one sunny morning. "When we set out I did not believe that Jesus Christ is the Son of God, and when we reached the zoo I did."[14] Yet the journey was neither thoughtful nor emotional; Lewis just suddenly possessed a simple, but great conviction.

The trip to the Whipsnade Zoo occurred on 28 September 1931, when Lewis was almost thirty-three years old. Meanwhile his father had died, and he and the Moores (Mrs. Moore and her daughter Maureen) set up housekeeping at the Kilns, where he was to spend the rest of his life. Soon Major Warren Lewis was to join them and to become in his own right a scholar of early modern to seventeenth century French history.

The first book to appear following Lewis's conversion was *The Pilgrim's Regress: An Allegorical Apology for Christianity, Reason and Romanticism* (May 1933). *The Pilgrim's Regress* sold 680 copies of the 1,000 printed. It was written during the two week period that Lewis spent in Belfast as a house guest of Arthur Greeves, and is an allegory in the style of Bunyan's *Pilgrim's Progress*. The main character is a sort of Everyman who, having tasted Joy, embarks on a long journey to rediscover it, only to learn that it could have been found in his own backyard. In a later edition, Lewis stated the theme as follows: "If a man diligently followed this desire [for Joy], pursuing the false objects until their falsity appeared and then resolutely abandoning them, he must come out at last into the clear knowledge that the human soul was made to enjoy some object that is never fully given . . . in our present mode of subjective and spatio-temporal existence."[15]

In the view of this writer, *The Pilgrim's Regress* is one of Lewis's best works, in spite of some obvious shortcomings. It is occasionally obscure, it is sometimes harsh and bitter in its characterizations, its poetry is not always a plus value and it is sometimes obtrusive in its classical learning. Nonetheless, it is a profound allegory which is at the same time delightful reading; it reveals a sharp wit and contains biting satire, and if it seems somewhat black and white in its interpretation of the Zeitgeist, much of this can be excused on the ground that it is the *apologia pro vita sua* of a recent convert endowed with a fervent earnestness.

Although Lewis is best known for his books on Christianity, it must be remembered that he was a professional scholar with a specialty in medieval and renaissance English literature. Christian apologetics was actually a sideline—the hobby which made him famous. His next major work *The Allegory of Love: A Study in Medieval Tradition* was in his field of expertise. Published in the spring of 1936, it was hailed as a first-rate piece of scholarship. "The book," Lewis said, "as a whole has two themes: 1. The birth of allegory and its growth from what it is in Prudentius to what it is in Spenser. 2. The birth of the romantic conception of love and the long struggle between its earlier form (the romance of adultery) and its later form (the romance of marriage)."[16] The book is a fine example of penetrating and exhaustive literary scholarship, but its appeal is limited and enjoys nothing like the popularity of the Christian writings. Still, it did establish Lewis as a scholar of the first magnitude.

Lewis was a highly organized person who disliked wasting time. He generally rose at 7:00 or 7:15, bathed, shaved, and took a turn on Addison's Walk. At 8:00 he attended matins in Magdalen Chapel, and breakfasted at 8:15. Breakfast was unhurried but was usually over by 8:25. From 9:00 to 1:00 he conducted tutorials, lunched and took a walk, returning to college at 4:45. Tutoring continued for another two hours, and at 7:15 he had dinner. He was generally in bed by 11:00. Lewis was extremely popular as a lecturer. He not infrequently borrowed someone's watch, lectured in a booming voice for forty-five minutes with astonishing erudition and a delightful wit, returned the borrowed watch as he gathered up his notes and concluded on the dot. Tutorials were apt to be somewhat overpowering. Lewis listened to prepared papers by his students and then criticized their style and content. Although he tried always to be charitable, he sometimes seemed a formidable tutor. Evenings were spent either at university clubs or with a small group of students in his rooms.

Occasionally informal meetings were limited to good friends, members of the Inklings. Among the things they talked about and criticized were the books they were writing. They delighted in the double entendre. Humphrey Carpenter has delineated some of the more important members in his book *The Inklings*, and Jocelyn Gibb's *Light on C. S. Lewis* and James Como's *C. S. Lewis at the Breakfast Table* contain a wealth of amusing and interesting personal detail on the Oxford don seen in this milieu.

In 1938 *Out of the Silent Planet* appeared as the first of the space trilogy novels. Its principal aim is to transfer certain theological questions to the planet Mars, where two evil scientists and one Christian work out their destinies among strange but splendid creatures who have not been contaminated by original sin. The silent planet is, of course, earth, which has been sealed off from the rest of the universe and is under the evil domination of the bent Oyarsa. Among other things, Lewis presents a shrewd insight into the nature of sin and evil and their effect on terrestrial creation. In a letter dated July 9, 1939, he wrote: "The danger of 'Westonism' [atheistic science] I meant to be real. What set me about writing the book was the discovery that a pupil of mine took all that dream of interplanetary colonization quite seriously, and the realization that thousands of people in one way and another depend on some hope of perpetuating and improving the human race for the whole meaning of the universe—that a 'scientific' hope of defeating death is a real rival to Christianity. You will be both grieved and amused to hear that out of about sixty reviews only two showed any knowledge that my idea of the fall of the Bent One was anything but an invention of my own . . . any amount of theology can now be smuggled into people's minds under cover of romance without their knowing it."[17]

Perelandra (Voyage to Venus), the second volume of the trilogy, did not appear until 1943, and the concluding volume, *That Hideous Strength*, came in 1945. In *Perelandra*, the first two rational creatures have just appeared and are still innocent. Ransom, the hero, arrives just in time to prevent their "falling." Where earth failed, Venus succeeds. The novel concludes with a superb Te Deum in which all the creatures of Venus praise the goodness of Maleldil (Christ). The depictions of the golden sky, the violent rainstorms, the floating islands, the huge waves and the Green Lady (who is a kind of blend of the Blessed Virgin and a pagan goddess) constitute some of Lewis's finest descriptive writing. The work is clearly inspired by Milton's *Paradise Lost*.

That Hideous Strength is indebted to Charles Williams, whom Lewis met in the fall of 1939. In his writing, Williams tended to combine the ordinary with the extraordinary; Lewis's novel is set in a contemporary English university town upon which unusual forces for both good and evil converge. It introduces a dead man's head kept alive by mechanical means, the ruthless N.I.C.E. (National Institute of Co-ordinated Experiments) and the sixth century wizard Merlin. Along the way there is the conversion of a woman named Jane Studdock and the gradual worldly disenchantment of her husband Mark. The characterization in this novel is excellent, particularly Wither, the bear Mr. Bultitude and, perhaps best of all, the memorable Fairy Hardcastle. The story winds up in a manner that certainly suggests either the end of the world or a great judgment of heaven. Lewis implies a triple conflict going on in the world, of grace against nature, and of nature against anti-nature. Although many scientists protested vigorously against *That Hideous Strength*, nonetheless it had good sales. After writing this splendid trilogy, Lewis never entered the field of science fiction again.

Rehabilitations and Other Essays appeared in 1939, as did *The Personal Heresy*, which contains Lewis's famous controversy with E. M. W. Tillyard. Lewis held for a classical interpretation of poetry—that it should be objective and impersonal with elevating subject matter. Tillyard, Master of Jesus College, Cambridge held for a more personal and subjective style, more in keeping with many of the romantics.

The disaster at Dunkirk in the spring of 1940 may have served as a backdrop for *The Problem of Pain*, published in October of that year. Lewis himself had already been called up for home guard duty. *The Problem of Pain* is a thorough exposition of the problem of human suffering. Why does a good God permit so much evil in the world? The book is almost a small summa, discussing as it does the nature of God and the fall of man, free will and its consequences, and the reality of heaven and hell. The most stimulating and most controversial chapter is on animal pain, where Lewis has no actual data and must "back into his subject" with considerable speculation and conjecture. The book was an enormous success and went through many editions, becoming one of the best statements of the problem of evil in modern times.

Invitations now came to preach. As early as 22 October 1939, he preached before the university in the Church of St. Mary the Virgin. His topic was "None Other Gods: Culture in War Time," in which he presented some of his thinking on the relationship between Christianity and culture. In 1941 he was appointed by the Royal Air Force as wartime lecturer on Christianity, and on 8 June 1941 he preached his famous sermon "The Weight of Glory" which was published in *Theology* the following November. On 6 August 1941 he gave the first of twenty-five talks on the BBC network which were to form the foundation of *Mere Christianity*. And in 1942, when the war was at its worst ("the year of dismay"), his most famous and popular book appeared: *The Screwtape Letters*.

Inspiration for *The Screwtape Letters* came one morning in church. Lewis wrote to his brother Warren: "After the service was over, I was struck by an idea for a book which I think might be both useful and entertaining. It would be called 'As One Devil to Another' and would consist of letters from an elderly retired devil to a young devil who has just started work on his first 'patient.' The idea would be to give all the psychology of temptation from the *other* point of view."[18] *The Screwtape Letters* was an enormous success and made Lewis both famous and affluent overnight. Yet he never considered it his best book, and although it was easily written, it was not for him an enjoyable work.

Walter Hooper (who seems almost to apologize for Lewis's belief in devils) states in his biography that Lewis's model for his book was Stephen McKenna's *Confessions of a Well-Meaning Woman* (1922), but the resemblance is tenuous at best.[19] The *Letters* would seem to be the result of years of study in moral and ascetical theology, but Lewis averred that in order to understand wickedness he needed only to consult his own heart. The considerable revenues from the book caused Owen Barfield to set up a charitable trust for Lewis into which two-thirds of all his royalties found their way.

Perhaps to offset what some scholars must have thought a frivolous publication, Lewis published the same year his *Preface to Paradise Lost*. It must be remembered that there were some at Oxford who thought Lewis should spend more time on scholarly publications and less time defending Christianity. His *Preface* would, therefore, be considered more important to his scholarly development and prestige than the *Letters*. It was felicitous that these publications should appear at approximately the same time.

Mere Christianity, published in 1952, was the final collection of the revised talks given over the BBC. It is actually three books put into one: *The Case for Christianity* (1943), *Christian Behaviour* (1943) and *Beyond Personality* (1945). Lewis was attempting in his talks to give a sort of overall summary of the Christian faith. Listeners report that the impact was tremendous. His style was always crystal clear, and he managed to summarize a very great deal of material in a short space of time. Traditional Christianity was being presented in a unique and compelling manner.

Mere Christianity is the best statement of Lewis's theological and moral position. It is a handy enchiridion, a brief but fairly complete summa of the Christian faith. Green and Hooper say that it is the one book of Lewis's to take along if stranded on a desert island, "Believing, as Lewis did," they continue, "that 'all that is not eternal is eternally out of date,' he never hedged, reinterpreted or in any way diluted the 'faith once given to the saints.' However modern or unusual the dress of his apologetics, Lewis was a thoroughgoing supernaturalist who appealed to the reason as well as the imagination in explaining the Incarnation, Christ's effectual sacrifice, the Resurrection, the Trinity, Heaven and Hell and the eternal seriousness of Christian decision."[20] But the book does have some shortcomings. It is weak on the sacraments, it is weak on the nature of the Church, and it is weak on the ideas of apostolic succession and the teaching magisterium.

Lewis's real strength lay in apologetics, and for this reason he was the guiding spirit of the Socratic Club at Oxford and its president for twenty-two years. This enormously popular club was a kind of arena of debate for Christians and atheists, or believers and non-believers, and between 1942 and 1953 Lewis presented no less than eleven formal papers there. The gist of his apologetic thrust was embodied in part in his *Abolition of Man* (1943), three lectures given at Durham University on the present state of education in the schools. *The Abolition of Man* attacks the idea that all moral and aesthetic values are subjective. Through a comparative study of many differing cultures, Lewis seeks to show that there has been an objective moral standard recognized throughout the ages—a Tao or Way. It is something we perceive rationally, not instinctively, and it is universally accepted.

The Great Divorce appeared in 1945. The idea underlying this delightful book is that suffering souls in hell may on occasion have periods of refreshment from eternal suffering—or a holiday from hell. Several people from hell take a bus excursion to see what heaven is like. With one exception, they all decide that hell is preferable. The exception occurs when a man with a lizard on his shoulder finally allows an angel to kill the lustful desires which the lizard represents. The lizard then turns into a magnificent stallion and the two ride off into deep heaven. The description of the incident is masterfully done; Lewis is at his finest here, and nowhere else in all his writings does he ever surpass this incident. *The Great Divorce* could conceivably be his greatest work.

In 1946 Lewis was awarded a Doctor of Divinity degree from Saint Andrew's University in Scotland, and he published an anthology of George MacDonald's work. Meanwhile, he was working on his next book, *Miracles*. *Miracles* is a difficult book, written for a very intellectual audience, and is probably one of Lewis's least popular works. Subtitled *A Preliminary Study*, it moves with less assurance than some of his previous writings. Miss G. E. M. Anscombe, the Roman Catholic philosopher, took sharp issue with some of Lewis's ideas about miracles, causing him to rethink and rewrite certain sections of the third chapter. There seems to be an element of uncertainty and inconclusiveness about the study, but it must be remembered that he labelled it "preliminary."

Three years after the death of Charles Williams, Lewis published as a commemoration the *Arthurian Torso: Containing the Posthumous Fragment of "The Figure of Arthur" by Charles Williams and a Commentary on the Arthurian Poems of Charles Williams by C. S. Lewis.* The book is very scholarly and has only a limited appeal to those interested in the Arthurian legend. The following year, 1949, saw a collection of Lewis's essays published under the title *Transposition and Other Addresses*, but the American edition, *The Weight of Glory and Other Addresses*, highlights the best of the essays. In the same year, Chad Walsh brought the attention of the American public to Lewis in his *C. S. Lewis: Apostle to the Skeptics*.

Roger Green was closely associated with Lewis at the time he was composing *Chronicles of Narnia*. In fact, it was Green who suggested this title for the septology. *The Lion, the Witch and the Wardrobe* appeared in 1950 and the rest followed at yearly intervals: *Prince Caspian, The Voyage of the "Dawn Treader," The Silver Chair, The Horse and His Boy, The Magician's Nephew* and, finally, *The Last Battle* (1956).

Opinions of the *Chronicles* are somewhat mixed. The best are *The Lion, the Witch and the Wardrobe* and *The Last Battle*. At least these two are the most obviously Christian. Many feel that the *Chronicles* establish Lewis as one of the greatest writers of children's books, while others feel that they are dull, not well-written and even, at times, condescending. Lewis's knowledge of actual children was slight, and this fact may be discernible in the books. It is certainly true that Lewis was not very interested in children— he wrote for himself and said so. The popularity of the *Chronicles* grew after his death, and it was perhaps greater in America than in England. This is interesting because the stories all have an English "flavor" and English expressions unfamiliar to Americans. Green and Hooper think that their popularity may someday surpass that of *The Screwtape Letters*, but this judgment seems extravagant.[21] It is a pity that they did not consider L. Frank Baum's *Oz* books for possible comparison. Perhaps the final evaluation should be left to children themselves; the books' general effect on adults seems to this writer to be on the whole ambivalent.

The prime minister offered Lewis the honor of Commander of the Order of the British Empire in 1951, but he refused this on grounds both personal and political. The following year he was awarded the honorary degree of Doctor of Literature by Laval University in Quebec, but did not go to Canada to receive the degree. By now he was somewhat freer at home (Mrs. Moore had died early in 1951) and diligently working on *English Literature in the Sixteenth Century, Excluding Drama,* his contribution (volume 3) to the *Oxford History of English Literature* (the OHEL, he called it). The book was based on his Clark Lecture series at Trinity College, Cambridge, and although it excludes drama from consideration, it is one of Lewis's finest pieces of scholarship. It was published in 1954.

Mention has already been made of Lewis's autobiography *Surprised by Joy* (1955), which describes his early life up to and including his conversion in 1931. It is an interesting self-analysis, coupled with a commentary on the British school system. It is also a splendid reminder that childhood and adolescent school days may not be the happiest times of our lives after all.

Lewis considered his novel *Till We Have Faces: A Myth Retold* his best work. The ancient legend of Cupid and Psyche is baptized and placed in a Christian framework. The main theme is Orual's psychological journey to self-realization and a conversion that helps her to understand the meaning of the world correctly. Until we have achieved our destiny, we may be said to be faceless, and for that reason the Gods cannot recognize us "till we have faces." It is not an easy novel and requires several readings to plumb its depths. It is quite unlike anything else Lewis wrote, and therefore it tends to "put people off." Yet it contains a combination of beauty and profundity rarely matched in any of his other works.

Tapes are in existence of Lewis reading from his *The Four Loves* (1960), which is an acute analysis of affection (storge), friendship (philia), eros, and charity (agape). Drawing very heavily from his own personal experience, Lewis once again presents a sort of summary of the Christian faith. This book is another fine example of the unique way he deals with traditional subject matter, adding insights and wit in an imaginative manner characteristic of him alone.

Lewis's life as a bachelor ended in 1956 when he surprised virtually everyone by marrying Joy Davidman, a Jewish divorcee. They met in 1952, when Joy moved to Oxford to try to patch up a rapidly deteriorating marriage. She and her husband had been converted to Christianity partly through the influence of Lewis's writings. If the initiative for friendship was first on her part, it was not long before it was warmly reciprocated. However, Joy was very sick with what was eventually diagnosed as cancer of the bone. She also was faced with the threat of deportation in 1956, and to provide her and her two sons with British citizenship, Lewis married her in a legal ceremony. On 21 March 1957 an ecclesiastical marriage was performed by her hospital bed, and she was sent home to Kilns to end her days. Then, miraculously, her case was arrested and her health improved to such an extent that the Lewises were able to travel to Greece in the spring of 1960—a trip Joy had long wanted to make.

The brief period when Joy seemed well was one of the happiest in Lewis's life. The two delighted in each other's company, and she helped and inspired him in his work (she had been a poet of considerable merit and possessed a lively intelligence). When the end came (three months after their return from Greece) Lewis was shattered. He deemed his loss almost unbearable and his *A Grief Observed* (1961) is a poignant account of the tremendous cataclysm through which he passed. At first sight it seems almost a repudiation of his previous work, almost a total loss of faith, but it happily concludes with an affirmation of belief in spite of everything.

Following World War II, there was an attempt to broaden the curriculum in English schools and to subsidize a larger number of students seeking educational opportunities. At Oxford, there was a strong demand on the part of some students and faculty to update the curricular offerings, and especially to modernize the courses in English literature. Lewis was opposed to this, fearing that education was being watered down and that practicality and technical knowledge were undermining the traditional course content. There came the increasing feeling among some of the faculty that Lewis was blocking any attempt at reform and was a stuffy old diehard. Envy no doubt played its part. In 1947 Lewis was passed over for the Merton Chair of English Literature; in 1951 he was defeated for the Professorship of Poetry. Finally in 1955 he accepted the Professorship of Medieval and Renaissance Literature at Magdalene College in Cambridge. Soon after, Oxford gave him an honorary fellowship, but the entire incident was an unfortunate one.

Lewis had no interest in and was often unaware of departmental power struggles and petty university politics. He was too big a man to realize that some of his colleagues might be envious. For their part, it could be argued that Lewis had not devoted a sufficient amount of his time and energy to scholarly research; the books on Christianity which had made him famous were likewise resented by some. Fortunately, the change was a happy one for Lewis, and at Cambridge he declared that he had found many of the values (and much of Oxford as he knew it) which he feared were being forfeited at Oxford. He was to remain in Cambridge until 1963, when he resigned his position shortly before his death.

Reflections on the Psalms appeared in 1958 and is said to have been greatly aided by the advice and expertise of Joy Davidman. It is Lewis's only book of Scripture commentary, although he was active on liturgical commissions for the revision of the psalter used in the Anglican Church. His *Studies in Words* was published in 1960, and a year later *An Experiment in Criticism*. He decided also to bring together his lectures on medieval and renaissance literature, but because of publication delays *The Discarded Image* did not appear until 1964, after his death. Another work not published during his lifetime was *Letters to Malcolm: Chiefly on Prayer*, which represents a kind of devotional summing up. (Malcolm is a ficticious character.) The *Letters* are both discerning and profound, updating the thought of such Anglican spiritual writers as William Laud and Jeremy Taylor. Their very personal and intimate style provides a special charm. During this last period, Lewis's essays and papers were being collected and published in book form. *They Asked for a Paper* (1962) is one such collection.

In July of 1963, Lewis's health steadily worsened; on the fifteenth he sank into a coma. He was given Extreme Unction with the expectation that he would die at any moment, but to the surprise of all he revived some hours later and in August returned to the Kilns with a male nurse. Although his health continued to improve, it was obvious that he was living on borrowed time. He resigned his professorship at Cambridge and, with the help of Walter Hooper (who had become Lewis's secretary as well as his close friend), began to put his affairs in order. He continued to receive numerous visitors well into November. November 22 began no differently from any other day, but at five-thirty P.M. his brother Warren heard a crash in the bedroom and ran in to find him lying unconscious at the foot of the bed. He died a few minutes later. Had he lived a week longer, he would have reached his sixty-fifth birthday.

C. S. Lewis was a preeminent literary scholar, but he was far better known for his Christian apologetics, and it is in this area that he will live on. This book attempts to survey some of his major theological ideas and to assess some of the contributions to contemporary Christian thinking that made him one of the most widely known, most popular and most beloved writers of the twentieth century.

2
God as God

C. S. Lewis never intends in his writing to make startling or original contributions to Christian thought; his aim throughout is to present "mere Christianity" from the standpoint of the layman. He avoids as far as possible controversial issues which might tend to befuddle the average man in the pew. But what *is* startling or original is the manner of presentation of time-honored truth; at this he is a genius.

We can begin to examine Lewis's writings by seeing how he views the one God, the "I Am" of Exodus 3:14. For Lewis, God is definitely not the amorphous spirit of pantheism. He strongly emphasizes the fact that God is concrete and individual. "He is 'absolute being'—or rather *the* Absolute Being—in the sense that He alone exists in His own right. But there are things which God is not. In that sense He has a determinate character. Thus He is righteous, not a-moral; creative, not inert. The Hebrew writings here observe an admirable balance. Once God says simply I AM, proclaiming the mystery of self-existence. But times without number He says, 'I am the Lord'—I, the ultimate Fact, have *this* determinate character and not *that*. And men are exhorted to 'know the Lord,' to discover and experience this particular character."[1]

Following in the tradition of Pseudo-Dionysius and John Scotus Erigena, Lewis lays considerable emphasis on the negative way in his discussion of God's attributes. We can say of each created thing that this is God, but we must also say neither is this God. "Neti, neti," says the Hindu mystic, "God is not thus." This is not to say that no positive statements about God are possible. We do not strip God of human attributes to leave him naked, but rather to make room for the insertion of positive divine attributes. We are limited in this, of course, by both our insight and our human language. To stand before God is to be confronted by the incomprehensible. "He is unspeakable not by being indefinite but by being too definite for the unavoidable vagueness of language. . . . Grammatically the things we say of Him are 'metaphorical': but in a deeper sense it is our physical and psychic energies that are mere 'metaphors' of the real Life which is God."[2]

Yet in the devotional and moral life, we constantly bump up against something concrete, and the growing emptiness of our idea of God is gradually filled with something definite. "Great prophets and saints have an intuition of God which is positive and concrete in the highest degree. Because, just touching the fringes of His being, they have seen that He is plentitude of life and energy and joy, therefore (and for no other reason) they have to pronounce that He transcends those limitations which we call personality, passion, change, materiality, and the like. The positive quality in Him which repels these limitations is the only ground for all the negatives."[3]

What definite qualities, then, does Lewis attribute to God? First, following in the footsteps of Saint Thomas Aquinas, he declares that God is omnipotent. But we must realize in what this omnipotence consists. It does not mean that God can do things which are intrinsically impossible. To ask if God could make a stone too heavy for Him to lift is to ask a meaningless question. Not even

God can make a square circle nor can He make something not to exist which has at some time existed. Of course it is possible for God to perform miracles, but He can never perform nonsense.[4]

What God does perform is always the work of a consummate artist. At the end of *Perelandra*, there is a paean of great praise for the Creator, who has planned the universe with such skill that it seems planless. Where no center seems to exist, we discover that all is center because everything is interlocked with everything else. Perfect goodness and perfect wisdom conspire to produce the best possible universe in the best possible way. God is absolutely free to produce whatever he wants, and to do it in whatever way he wants. And when we speak of the divine goodness, we are not speaking of something that is totally alien to human goodness. Although Lewis prefers the word *metaphor*, he borrows heavily from the Thomistic doctrine of *analogy*. God is good as humans can be good, but God's greatness is above any finite experience of human goodness we can know.[5]

Lewis's concept of God's majesty is expressed in superb imagery in his fiction, as this passage from *That Hideous Strength* demonstrates: "Kingship and power and festal pomp and courtesy shot from him as sparks fly from an anvil. The pealing of bells, the blowing of trumpets, the spreading out of banners, are means used on earth to make a faint symbol of his quality. It was like a long sunlit wave, creamy-crested and arched with emerald, that comes on nine feet tall, with roaring and with terror and unquenchable laughter. It was like the first beginning of music in the halls of some King so high and at some festival so solemn that a tremor akin to fear runs through young hearts when they hear it. For this was great Glund-Oyarsa, King of Kings, through whom the joy of creation blows across these fields of Arbol."[6]

The majesty of God is only dimly reflected in his creation of the universe, created freely out of absolutely nothing. Using the triune formula of Father, Redeemer, and indwelling Comforter, Lewis shows that the universe is small indeed compared with Ultimate Reality; so how much smaller earth is when compared to the universe, and man when compared to the earth. This is not designed to produce a despair of man's pitiful smallness, as Pascal also made clear, but simply to say that all this is nothing against "the intolerable light of utter actuality."[7]

Important attributes of God are his justice and mercy, which are one in him but different from our perspective. Consciously or not, Lewis again makes use of the Thomistic doctrine that such attributes can be predicated from the human standpoint because they have a foundation in reality. He likewise treats of God's wrath and God's pardon in this way. Of course, applied to God these are metaphors; but we must be aware of what Scripture tells us, and certainly God's anger can be a consuming fire. Yet the reverse side of the coin is his mercy, which is tender, loving and forgiving to the blotting out of sins. Lewis always reminds us that when we speak of the attributes of God, we speak in a supereminent fashion. What God is in actuality is simply beyond all human imagination. God is his mercy and much more; God is his justice and much more than "eye hath seen or ear heard" (cf. 1 Cor. 2:9).

In *Reflections on the Psalms*, Lewis writes, "There were in the eighteenth century terrible theologians who held that 'God did not command certain things because they are right, but certain things are right because God commanded them.' To make the position perfectly clear, one of them even said that though God has, as it happens, commanded us to love Him and one another, He might equally well have commanded us to hate Him and one another, and hatred would then have been right."[8] Lewis rejects this voluntaristic approach to God. God can be no other than what he is: absolute goodness, justice, mercy and love. And he is all of these supereminently, as we have just said.

We need to say a word now about Lewis's view of God's government of the universe. He refers to the vision of Lady Julian (in which God carried in his hand a little object like a nut which represented all creation) to make the point that governing the universe is no great task for God. Being all-sufficient in himself, God still loves into existence the superfluous, since he is almost overflowing with goodness. This is not to be understood in the Neo-Platonic sense, for God is under no compulsion to create anything. He creates and conserves in existence so that he can love all created being.[9]

This brings us to a consideration of God's love. We are not to construe it as something sentimental, or something which excites our feelings. We have a Father in heaven, but not a benevolent grandfather who simply wants everyone to have a good time on earth. God's love is pure, spiritual and intellectual, and quite unlike the love we generally experience; there may be almost an element of ferocity about it. In a word, God is exacting in his love; we are happy only insofar as this is compatible with praising, reverencing and serving him. He is not concerned about people's saying at the end of the day, "A good time was had by all." He is not to be mistaken for mere kindness, because he has loved us to the utmost.

In *The Problem of Pain* (Chapter 3), we come face to face with God's love and human suffering. Each one of us is a divine work of art, and the Heavenly Artist has paid us the "intolerable compliment" of creating us in his image. Nor will he rest until he has accomplished his will, until each of us grows in Godlikeness according to the plan he has laid out for us. We may not altogether like the infinite care and patience which go into our artistry, but Lewis points out that in wishing for a less glorious and a less arduous destiny, we are asking not for more love but for less. Here is an illustration from the canine world: "In [the dog's] state of nature it has a smell, and habits, which frustrate man's love: he washes it, house-trains it, teaches it not to steal, and is so enabled to love it completely. To the puppy the whole proceeding would seem, if it were a theologian, to cast grave doubts on the 'goodness' of man: but the full-grown and full-trained dog, larger, healthier, and longer-lived than the wild dog; and admitted, as it were by Grace, to a whole world of affections, loyalties, interests, and comforts entirely beyond its animal destiny, would have no such doubts."[10]

Our God is a consuming fire, a tremendous lover, a passionate seeker after every individual. He is the Lord of the terrible aspect, and to look upon him face to face is to die. We must not sentimentalize this God. He is "not a senile benevolence that drowsily wishes you to be happy in your own way, not the cold philanthropy of a conscientious magistrate, nor the care of a host who feels responsible for the comfort of his guests.[11]

We are not the center of the universe; God is its center and all things—man included—exist for God. Hence God cannot allow us to remain as we are; his love constantly seeks to enlarge the mansion of our soul, for it is in this mansion that he intends to live himself. In answer to the question, Have I a right to be happy? God replies no. Sin has marred our character to such an extent that God must cajole, woo, threaten, refashion, and redesign our inner selves to his satisfaction, not our own. To struggle against this, to throw up blocks, to fail to surrender the fort, is once again (in one of Lewis's favorite expressions) to ask for less love, not for more.

One of the basic doctrines of Christianity is that God is three-Personed, while still remaining one Being. When an ordinary Christian says his prayers, he is aware that there is Something in him encouraging him to pray and Someone alongside of him directing that prayer to an Other who is the object of the prayer.

While the three Persons of the Godhead constitute one Being, nevertheless each Person is God, and is equated with the total Godhead. And while we refer to them as Persons, this is only by analogy, for each is supereminently a person. In fact, the better terminology is Father, Son and Holy Spirit, and these are terms which are relations as much as Persons. Lewis's best statement of the Trinity is in the concluding section of *Mere Christianity*. He aptly titles this part "Beyond Personality," since our human language is not adequate to these great truths.

The Father begets the Son. This is neither a causal relationship nor a temporal one. The Father does not make the Son, because what is made is always unlike its maker, whereas what is begotten has a parental likeness. This begetting occurs outside of time; there never was when the Son did not exist. The Father takes delight in his Son; the Son looks up to his Father. But this has always been so. In fact, we do not know what is meant by "begotten of the Father"; we only know that this is a true statement. Saint Gregory Nazianzus tells us that if we could explain these statements, we should be locked up in a madhouse.

The Holy Spirit (the third Person) seems to be somewhat vaguer to most people than either the Father or the Son. Lewis explains it by first telling us that God is love. This is a commonly accepted Christian statement. It has ramifications, however, because the words have no real meaning unless God implies at least two Persons. Love is something that one person has for another; it is a flow between lover and object and back. If God was a single Person, then before the world was made, he was not love. Of course, often when people say that God is love, they mean that love is God. They are saying that our feelings of love are to be treated with great respect. Granting the validity of this, it is not what Christianity teaches when it says God is love. The Christian belief is that "the living, dynamic activity of love has been going on in

God forever and has created everything else."[12] The love is the love between the Father and the Son.

What develops out of the joint life of the Father and Son is the third of the three Persons who are God. We say that the Lover (the Father) loves the Beloved (the Son) and the Beloved loves the Lover so both generate the Love (the Holy Spirit) which passes between them. And the Holy Spirit acts through us. If the Father is "out there" in front of us, and the Son is standing by our side, guiding us to become another son, then the third Person is working within us. "God is love, and that love works through men—especially the whole community of Christians. But this spirit of love is, from all eternity, a love going on between the Father and the Son."[13]

To conclude our discussion of Lewis's view of the nature of God, we need to examine some of the attributes he gives to Christ. Christ is actually the main character in *The Chronicles of Narnia*, though he appears in the guise of a lion named Aslan. This fictional portrayal of the Lord is masterfully done and gives us a fair understanding of Lewis's concept of him. We first hear about Aslan in *The Lion, the Witch and the Wardrobe*, when the four children from our world have taken refuge in the Narnian home of Mr. and Mrs. Beaver.

"Is—is he a man?" asked Lucy.

"Aslan a man!" said Mr. Beaver sternly. "Certainly not. I tell you he is the King of the wood and the son of the great Emperor-Beyond-the-Sea. Don't you know who is the King of Beasts? Aslan is a lion—*the* Lion, the great Lion."

"Ooh" said Susan, "I'd thought he was a man. Is he—quite safe? I shall feel rather nervous about meeting a lion."

"That you will, dearie, and no mistake," said Mrs. Beaver, "if there's anyone who can appear before Aslan without their knees knocking, they're either braver than most or else just silly."

"Then he isn't safe?" said Lucy.

"Safe?" said Mr. Beaver. "Don't you hear what Mrs. Beaver tells you?
Who said anything about safe? 'Course he isn't safe. But he's good.
He's the King, I tell you."[14]

The royal nature of Aslan (Christ) emerges first, for he is the
son of the great Emperor (the Father). This is part of Lewis's
trinitarian formula; later he will refer to the Holy Spirit as "The
Third One." We also learn at once that Aslan is not "safe"; he is
not a *tame* lion. This is one of Lewis's favorite themes. Just as it
is a fearful thing to fall into the hands of the living God, so it is
no less fearful to confront Aslan. One will not merely be nervous,
one's knees will knock. When people were confronted by Christ
during his earthly life, they generally felt hatred, terror or adoration. Ever on guard against a too sentimental interpretation of
Christianity, Lewis likes to underscore the reaction of terror. But
the Beavers also insist that Aslan is good, and since he is good,
he is lovable.

While this discussion is going on at the Beavers', one of the
children, Edmund, takes the opportunity of sneaking out and making his way to the White Witch. She successfully lures him with
Turkish Delight, and before long claims him as her prize. He will-
ingly betrays Aslan. This results in a confrontation between Aslan
and the witch at the Stone Table, and the subsequent death by torture of Aslan followed by his resurrection. How is it that in the
end the nefarious plans of the Evil One are frustrated? It is because her knowledge of the "Deep Magic" goes back only to the
dawn of time. "But if she could have looked a little further back,"
Aslan explains, "into the stillness and the darkness before Time
dawned, she would have read there a different incantation. She
would have known that when a willing victim who had committed
no treachery was killed in a traitor's stead, the Table would crack
and Death itself would start working backwards."[15] This is Lewis's
capsule interpretation of the Redemption; here we need to notice

that Aslan has existed before the dawn of time, that he is the sinless but willing victim killed in the place of the traitor, and that he is willing to die for a single traitor. His actions result in destroying death itself, in causing it to begin to work backwards. The writing here is some of Lewis's finest.

In *Prince Caspian*, the fundamental role of Aslan is to guide others. Because the children have not followed their first vision of him, Aslan becomes invisible to all but Lucy, who discovers that he is bigger than when she last saw him. That is because she is older, he tells her. Every year that she grows, she will find him bigger. Thus the immensity of God is demonstrated as well.[16] The following of Christ must take place regardless of opposition, including that of one's own family. Lucy is the youngest of the four children, and when your older brothers and sisters oppose you, that can be formidable opposition.

The "guide" or "shepherd" aspect of God (for if the lion is the king of beasts, he can also be called their shepherd) is repeated in *The Silver Chair*, when Puddleglum says, "There are no accidents [accidental happenings]. Our Guide is Aslan."[17] We see that human affairs are often directed by a higher Wisdom. God as both Lawgiver and One obedient to his own rules is suggested in *The Voyage of the "Dawn Treader,"* when Aslan tells Lucy that she has just made him visible. "Do you think I wouldn't obey my own rules?" he demands of her, indicating that he is just as much bound by the Tao as his own creation.[18] Since God obeys his own law, man must obey as well.

The story of doubting Thomas in Saint John's resurrection account is translated into equestrian terms in *The Horse and His Boy*. Aslan says to the horse, Bree,

"You poor, proud, frightened Horse, draw near. Nearer still, my son. Do not dare not to dare. Touch me. Smell me. Here are my paws, here is my tail, these are my whiskers. I am a true Beast."

"Aslan," said Bree in a shaken voice. "I'm afraid I must be rather a fool."

"Happy the Horse who knows that while he is still young. Or the Human either."[19]

Here we have an insistence on the "bestial" qualities of Aslan, whose nature is divine as well—two natures in one animal. One glance at the lion's face is sufficient to cause an act of self-prostration. As a matter of fact, this is exactly what happens to Shasta a few chapters earlier. "But after one glance at the Lion's face, he slipped out of the saddle and fell at its feet. . . . The High King above all kings stooped towards him. . . . He lifted his face and their eyes met. Then instantly the pale brightness of the mist and the fiery brightness of the Lion rolled themselves together into a swirling glory and gathered themselves up and disappeared."[20]

But there are occasions when Aslan registers disapproval or even anger by a low growl, sometimes accompanied by a lashing of the tail. This generally occurs when an act of disobedience has been, or is about to be, committed. Early in *The Silver Chair*, Jill meets Aslan sitting by a stream of water:

"Are you not thirsty?" said the Lion.

"I'm dying of thirst," said Jill.

"Then drink," said the Lion.

"May I—could I—would you mind going away while I do?" said Jill.

The Lion answered this only by a look and a very low growl. . . .

"I daren't come and drink," said Jill.

"Then you will die of thirst," said the Lion.

"Oh dear!" said Jill, coming another step nearer. "I suppose I must go and look for another stream then."

"There is no other stream," said the Lion.[21]

Aslan also plays the role of helper, protector or rescuer in several of the Narnia chronicles. In *The Voyage of the "Dawn*

Treader," Eustace has turned into a dragon and will remain that
way until Aslan breaks the spell by ripping the scales from the
selfish boy.[22] In *The Horse and His Boy*, Aslan protects Shasta
and Bree by walking by their side (unknown to them) to prevent
them from falling down a chasm.

The creation of Narnia, and hence the first of *The Chronicles*
if one is to take them in temporal sequence, is described in *The
Magician's Nephew*. Here Aslan calls into existence (sings, properly) his created world, and then from this created world chooses
(quite apart from their intrinsic merit) dancing trees, talking
beasts—exceptionally gifted creatures. Evil has entered this world
as well, and Aslan cautions his creatures in the very early hours
about the need to keep Narnia safe from it. It is as creator, pre-
server, gift-giver and restorer that Aslan appears here.

We can conclude this section with a consideration of Aslan's
attributes as they are revealed in *The Last Battle*. Here he appears
as consummator and judge. Lucy asks him to convince the dwarfs
that they must believe in him, but the dwarfs refuse to be taken
in. Their policy is one of strict neutrality between good and evil,
and their slogan is "The Dwarfs are for the Dwarfs." Aslan com-
mands a glorious feast to appear before them, but still the dwarfs
believe they are eating only what can be found in a barn. Aslan
cannot, will not, compel assent. "You see," he says, "they will not
let us help them. They have chosen cunning instead of belief.
Their prison is only in their own minds, yet they are in that
prison; and so afraid of being taken in that they can not be taken
out."[23]

At the destruction of Narnia, all of the creatures come rushing
up to Aslan; one or other of two things happens to each of them.
All look straight into his face, but those who look with fear and
hatred immediately swerve to the lion's left and disappear into his
huge black shadow. Others look with fear and love, and go into

the door on Aslan's right. A surprise awaits Emeth, who has always served the god Tash and hated the name of Aslan. He is rewarded by Aslan because of his fervor and devotion, in spite of the fact that he has served a false god. Lewis has already warned us in *The Screwtape Letters* that God rewards some for serving causes which he may disapprove of, for even in their ignorance such people have shown sincerity and devotion. Emeth is one of these people, and this whole idea is articulated at considerable length at the end (chapter 15) of *The Last Battle*.

Further up and further in (as Lewis charmingly puts it) is the call to those who have loved Aslan and are being rewarded by him. A new Narnia replaces the old Narnia which has been destroyed, and we are to understand that when Aslan rewards his followers, the rewards have just begun and will continue to increase indefinitely. *The Chronicles* conclude with these wonderful words: "All their life in this world and all their adventures in Narnia had only been the cover and the title page: now at last they are beginning Chapter One of the Great Story, which no one on earth has read: which goes on for ever: in which every chapter is better than the one before."[24]

God as Creator

Having considered God as he is in himself, in this next chapter we need to review Lewis's concept of God as Creator—of things visible and invisible. In the space trilogy, Lewis calls the Creator Maleldil the Young (God the Son). We are to understand that our world is only one of many worlds that he created, and our time only one of many possible times. This theme of different times for different worlds also runs through *The Chronicles of Narnia*. "Once you're out of Narnia," says Edmund in *Prince Caspian*, "you have no idea how Narnian time is going. Why shouldn't hundreds of years have gone past in Narnia while only one year has passed for us in England?"[1]

The true wonder and amazing variety of God's creation is experienced by Ransom, the hero of the space trilogy, as he travels to other worlds. The golden sky dome of Perelandra (Venus) and the abundance of water, islands and lush vegetation show him how parochial his former ideas have been. He is struck by this again when he meets the various types of rational beings on Malacandra (Mars): the sorns, hrossa, and pfifltriggi. The Oyarsa (ruling spirit) of Malacandra points out that both he and Ransom are copies of Maleldil, and we infer that the other "rational animals" are also reflections of the One who made the worlds.[2]

Since Maleldil made all the worlds and created time for each, it follows that he is outside these things. Hence, Lewis rejects both pantheism and naturalism and holds the Jewish-Christian concept of a God who stands outside of creation altogether. In fact, in his book on *Miracles* Lewis shows that naturalism is self-contradictory because it fails to account for man's ability to reason above nature, and indeed nature is not able to account for the moral law to which we all appeal at one time or another, even though we may not follow it.[3]

Creation is good, and shows God to be a very great artist indeed. Even fallen man is said to be good, for although the inhabitants of earth require redemption, still Screwtape reminds Wormwood that the Enemy "really likes the little vermin."[4] "He really does want to fill the universe with a lot of loathsome little replicas of Himself."[5] Their lives are to be qualitatively like his own, but on a miniature scale; somehow they are to be like him while still remaining themselves.

One of Lewis's favorite biblical texts is Psalm 16:11. "At thy right hand there are pleasures forevermore" is the King James translation. According to Screwtape, hell has not yet succeeded in creating one single pleasure, in spite of much diligent research. Pleasures, then, are one more example of the rich variety of God's creation. "It is misery enough," says Screwtape, "to see them in their mortal days taking off dirtied and uncomfortable clothes and splashing in hot water and giving little grunts of pleasure . . . ," but of course the greatest pleasure of all will be the final stripping, the complete cleansing at the time of death.[6] While Jonathan Edwards might not have written such a paean of pleasure, he would have agreed with Lewis's idea of worshipping the Lord in the beauty of holiness.

Although creation is basically good, it is not an eternal creation. Aristotle held for the eternity of the world, and St. Thomas Aquinas observed that the eternity of the world could be defended by reason, but revelation clearly teaches that the world is both created and finite. Or, more precisely, the world we perceive through our senses is both finite and temporal, while the real world, the invisible world, is not. Christians believe that some day the world as we know it is going to come to an end. And Lewis makes it very clear in the space trilogy that there will be a final showdown on earth, the troubled planet—perhaps very soon. When he is on Venus (Perelandra), Ransom is told by King Tor,

> "The seige of your world shall be raised, the black spot cleared away, before the real beginning. In those days Maleldil [God] will go to war —in us, and in many who once were *bnau* on your world, and in many from far off and in many eldila, and, last of all, in Himself unveiled, He will go down to Thulcandra. . . . And as Maleldil Himself draws near, the evil things in your world shall show themselves stripped of disguise so that plagues and horrors shall cover your lands and seas. But in the end all shall be cleansed, and even the memory of your Black Oyarsa blotted out, and your world shall be fair and sweet and reunited to the field of Arbol and its true name shall be heard again."[7]

What about God's human creation? Although the fact that man's basic nature is tainted, or has an inclination to evil, is granted by Lewis, he does not see it as totally depraved in the Calvinistic sense, or dangling over the fiery pit in the Edwardsian sense. Man is endowed with reason, a reason which is capable of transcending nature and also reaching much truth without the aid of revelation. Rational clarity is a gift of God, and Screwtape declares that "the trouble about argument is that it moves the whole struggle onto the Enemy's own ground. . . . By the very act of arguing, you awake the patient's reason; and once it is awake, who can foresee the result?"[8] Although Lewis is often thought of as a romantic (and rightly so), it cannot be emphasized too strongly that he was essentially a rationalist. He possessed a keenly-honed mind which could readily detect shoddy thinking. His thorough training in the classical languages and literature helped to enhance a first-rate intellect.

But man is also a creation of emotion. He lives with feelings as well as intellect, for these, too, are God-given. One of Lewis's major themes is the doctrine of yearning (Sehnsucht). It is prominent in all of his writings, but particularly in his first major and Christian work, *The Pilgrim's Regress.* This unarticulated longing, this desire, this homesickness which cannot be satisfied by anything on earth—not even human love—is one of his strongest proofs for the existence of God. It is the famous Augustinian dictum: "Our hearts are restless until they find their rest in Thee."[9] This "romantic" theme recurs again in *The Chronicles of Narnia* and in *Till We Have Faces,* but perhaps it is most clearly articulated in *Surprised by Joy.*

Man embraces a third component as a total human person—his power of will. Man is able to make choices, and it is his choices which ultimately lead him to the beatific vision or the miserific vision. What God wants is for man to choose him and to follow his will, even when any trace of God's presence has been removed from the universe. In the long run, there are only two kinds of people: those who say to God, "Thy will be done," and those to whom God says, "*Thy* will be done." Screwtape reminds Wormwood that it does not matter how the devil is to edge a man away from the Light and out into Nothing. "Murder," he says, "is no better than cards if cards can do the trick. Indeed, the safest road to Hell is the gradual one—the gentle slope, soft underfoot, without sudden turnings, without milestones, without signposts."[10]

Lewis does not deny the necessity of grace, but he does deny that we are so conditioned by our nature and our nurture that we are not capable of moral choices. The moral law impinges upon all, as Lewis has particularly indicated in *The Abolition of Man;* so that each one of us has a Kantian obligation to exercise this aspect of our practical reason. Lewis will have none of moral determinism, Freudian, Marxist or otherwise.

William Luther White in *The Image of Man in C. S. Lewis* thinks that the space trilogy throws much light on the question of what it means to be human by transporting three earth-men to Mars and Venus, thus forcing them into contrast with other rational beings. Unlike earth, Malacandra is not a "fallen" planet and enjoys a relationship with God which has not been clouded or marred by sin. What might our world have been like if sin had not corrupted it? The visits to both Mars and Venus set out to answer that question. Nor is the matter one of pure speculation. What if scientific exploration comes across just such worlds in the future? It would be folly to think that their inhabitants would be naive and without scientific sophistication. In *Out of the Silent Planet*, Lewis wishes to suggest just the opposite. In the "presentation before Oyarsa," the evil scientists from earth who think themselves sophisticated and wise emerge as colossal fools.

The human lot is also viewed in *The Chronicles of Narnia*. In *Prince Caspian*, Aslan says to the prince, "You come of the Lord Adam and the Lady Eve. And that is both honour enough to erect the head of the poorest beggar, and shame enough to bow the shoulders of the greatest emperor in earth. Be content."[11] Again in *Prince Caspian*, Lucy observes, "Wouldn't it be dreadful if some day in our own world, at home, men started going wild inside, like the animals here, and still looked like men, so that you'd never know which were which?"[12] Some think that has already happened!

We cannot leave a discussion of God's creation without examining Lewis's treatment of those pure beings we call angels. He refers to them in a number of his writings, but they are most fully depicted in the space trilogy. The eldila, as they are named here, populate the planet Mars, and Ransom learns from one of the

intelligent beings living on Mars that they are "hard to see. They
are not like us. Light goes through them. You must be looking in
the right place and at the right time; and that is not likely to come
about unless the *eldil* wishes to be seen. Sometimes you can mistake them for a sunbeam or even a moving of the leaves; but when
you look again you see that it was an *eldil* and that it is gone. But
whether your eyes can ever see them I do not know."[13]

Very soon we learn that eldila have bodies, although these
bodies are not necessarily material. They are bodies because they
have movement, and the speed of their movement determines
whether one smells something, or hears a sound, or sees a sight.
The body of an eldil moves as swiftly as the speed of light, but
Lewis reminds us that we do not truly see light, only slower things
lit by it; light is on the edge—the last thing we know before things
become too swift for us. In the Lewis cosmology, there is a reversal
of physics; what seems opaque to us is actually less substantial than
things like light or melody. To the eldila, what we call firm things
—flesh and earth—seem thinner and harder to see than our light,
and more like clouds, and nearly nothing.

In *The Great Divorce*, it was the blessed in heaven who were
substantial and "more real" than the shadowy visitors who had
come from hell and who could hardly stand on the sharp glass-like
grass because they were simply not solid enough. The same idea is
repeated in *Till We Have Faces;* sin and lack of self-surrender to
the will of God prevent us from becoming true individuals because
we are alienated from Reality. We need to acquire faces.

When Ransom arrives at the island where he is to meet the great
Oyarsa, he feels that the island is having a look at him. He becomes aware of tiny variations of light and shade; yet when he
concentrates on any particular spot, the minute brightness which
had attracted him seems to have just left. The sensation is not exactly uncanny; rather he has the impression of being looked at by
things that have a right to look. It is not fear that he feels, but a

combination of embarrassment, shyness and profound uneasiness. The presence of the eldila clearly makes Ransom uncomfortable.

Somewhat later, Ransom discovers that these invisible intelligences greatly outnumber the visible Malacandrians, who turn out to be the smallest part of the silent consistory that is surrounding him. The impression now becomes one of a large audience before whom one is about to act, to plead, or to attempt a justification of one's self. Then it occurs to Ransom that perhaps this waiting and being looked at was the actual trial, and that he was unconsciously telling the eldila all they wished to know. On the silent planet of earth (Thulcandra), the eldila are not known, and it is Ransom's opinion that they have never visited there. He becomes less certain of this, however, as he recalls the recurrent human tradition of the occasional appearance of bright elusive creatures that so far have been explained away by anthropologists.

Oyarsa may be said to be the archangel of the planet Malacandra. Maleldil (God) rules through him. The name "Maleldil" seems to suggest some sort of angel, but Lewis's intention is rather that Maleldil is the ruler of the angels—and of the whole universe. At any rate, the eldila on Malacandra obey Oyarsa, and their duty at the end of *Out of the Silent Planet* is to see the spaceship safely back to earth. On the voyage home, Ransom's confidence in Oyarsa's words about the eldila increases rather than diminishes. He never sees them, because the intensity of light in which the ship swims does not allow it. Yet he thinks he hears all sorts of delicate sounds or vibrations mixed with the tinkling rain of meteorites. Often the sense of unseen presences even within the spaceship becomes irresistible. The point to all this is that humans may be totally unaware of the true population of the universe, the three-dimensional infinitude of their territory, and the unchronicled aeons of the past. There are more things in heaven and earth than are dreamed of in our philosophy.

The eldila are reintroduced almost immediately in the second book of the trilogy, *Perelandra*. They have come to earth to summon Ransom to Venus. The narrator of the story—Lewis himself —wants nothing to do with these powerful supernatural intelligences. In a word, he does not wish to be "drawn in." To see the universe as populated by these beings is considered by most people to be a sign of madness (but perhaps those who see them are the only ones who see the world as it really is).

The central theme of *Perelandra* is the attempt of an evil scientist (Weston) to tempt Queen Tinidril into disobedience and corruption, and Ransom's effort to convince her not to listen. At times Weston loses his own personal identity and is overtaken by Satan himself. The temptation of the Lady is ultimately unsuccessful, and the remainder of the novel is occupied with a deadly struggle between Ransom and Weston, with the former the victor. There is general rejoicing as King Tor and Queen Tinidril hold court and then plan to send Ransom back to the silent planet. The eldila again figure prominently in this last scene, and they transport Ransom back to earth in the same mysterious and rather beautiful manner in which they brought him.

The ruling Oyarsa of the planet Venus is named Perelandra, and until this final scene her existence has not been known. "I was not set to rule over them," she explains with regard to the king and queen, although she ruled all else. "I rounded this ball when it first arose from Arbol. I spun the air about it and wove the roof. I built the Fixed Island and this, the holy mountain, as Maleldil taught me. The beasts that sing and the beasts that fly and all that swims on my breast and all that creeps and tunnels within me down to the centre has been mine. And today all this is taken from me. Blessed be He."[14]

That Hideous Strength concludes the trilogy. The first specific mention of the eldila occurs when Jane goes to the Director of St. Anne's in order to get help for her marriage. After a brief (and to moderns, unpopular) discussion on obedience as an erotic necessity, the Director tells her to return home and talk to her husband, while he will talk with his "authorities." They come to him when they please; so while talking to Jane, the Director is suddenly interrupted and he says gently, "Quick, you must leave now. This is no place for us small ones, but I am inured. Go!"[15]

Evil eldila are even now at work in England, and Bracton College is the scene of their endeavor. They have already taken possession of such persons as Lord Feverstone, Dr. Frost, Dr. Filostrato, the Rev. Fr. Straik and the notorious Fairy Hardcastle, a sadistic lesbian. Good eldila are not strictly planetary creatures, as Jane is told, but inhabitants of outer space (Deep Heaven). It is for their help that the Director is waiting. Ultimately the eldila arrive and contribute to the denouement of the book and the entire space trilogy.

This general overview indicates the role Lewis has the angels (eldila) play in the economy of the universe. He holds the interesting theory that when the world was younger, the division between matter and spirit had not become so clear as it is now. There used to be angels who were not guardian angels; they did not help humanity, but neither did they harm it. They simply went about their own business, and less sophisticated ages called them gods, elves, dwarfs, water-people, longaevi and so on. But the division between matter and spirit has now become more clear-cut, and this third division of neither-good-nor-evil spirits has been forced either to take sides or, more probably, has passed out of existence. This presents a problem, for if they have gone out of existence, then they were not aeviternal to start with; and if they have been forced to take sides, they seem to have taken on a human, or at least a moral, quality. Lewis does not develop this idea, perhaps because it is vague and is neither scientifically verified nor part of revelation.

How, then, does Lewis's doctrine of the eldila compare with
the traditional Christian doctrine on angels? Christianity has always
affirmed that at the beginning of time, God created spiritual es-
sences out of nothing. With this Lewis agrees, although nowhere
does he say they came out of nothing; this is implied. What Lewis
does stress is that there is an immeasurable host of angels, and in
Out of the Silent Planet this vast assembly far outnumbers the
flesh and blood creation. What interests him even more than their
number is their proximity to us and their concern for us. We are
surrounded by them; they are before and behind, and they populate the whole universe.

We have already said that they are more substantial than humans, that to Lewis the lighter things in the universe are more
substantial than the heavier, opaque, material things. Since the
angels are pure forms, they know things instantaneously, whereas
humans (impeded by matter, the principle of unintelligibility)
learn only through discursive reasoning, and laboriously at that.
Saint Thomas holds that each angel forms a separate species, since
an angel has no matter, and matter is the principle of individuation
in substance. His teacher, Albertus Magnus, however, believed that
all angels were of one species, while the Franciscan school and the
Jesuit theologian Suárez maintained that the individual hierarchies
or choirs form particular species.

Now a great number of the Church Fathers ascribed to the
angels a fine ethereal or firelike substance. Among them was Saint
Augustine, who had never quite rid himself of Stoic and Platonic
influences. Also, certain passages of Scripture seem to support this
view (Ps. 103:4 and Gen. 6:2). Yet other Fathers, such as Euse-
bius of Caesarea, Saint Gregory Nazianzus, Pseudo-Dionysius and
Saint Gregory the Great, insisted on the pure spirituality of angels.
But in the high Middle Ages, the Franciscan school applied the
hylomorphic composition of matter to spiritual created substances,

and this implied a kind of spiritual matter in the angelic substance. It is this latter theory to which Lewis seems to subscribe.

When Ransom becomes aware of the eldila on the island in Malacandra, he does more than sense their presence; he faintly sees Oyarsa himself. Does Lewis wish to imply that this is because there is a kind of light-substance that makes this possible, or does Oyarsa take on some accidental property which makes it possible for Ransom to detect the presence of one who is normally in pure form? Perhaps the point cannot be pushed too far, since we are dealing with a romantic fantasy rather than a theological summa; and even if Lewis does hold the Franciscan theory, that would by no means make him heretical!

The more common or Thomistic position is that when angels wish to be seen by men, they take on some special bodies for the purpose. This happened when the angels appeared to Abraham, when Raphael accompanied Tobias, when Gabriel was sent to Mary, when Adam and Eve were ejected from the Garden of Eden, and so on. It is hard to define Lewis's precise position here, since, as we have said, he is writing fiction and not theology.

In any case, he seems to view angels as an important and active part of God's creation. In the space trilogy, outer space is not cold, dark and bare. It is better described as "Deep Heaven," which is populated by innumerable benign beings (the good eldila, or angels) utterly devoted to God (Maleldil) and deeply concerned about the fate of human beings on this planet. In the final conflict which is sure to occur on Thulcandra (earth), the evil eldila (devils) really have no chance at all of winning. Lewis wants us to take the last battle seriously, even though it is only the prelude to "further up and further in."

4

Man's Problem: Man

Nothing is more obvious than the effect of original sin in the world; nothing is more difficult to prove. Many have commented on the dual nature of man: how like a god in so many things, and how like a beast in so many others. In fact, man can sink considerably lower than the beasts. It is one of the ironies of the twentieth century that we can put men on the moon while standing at the brink of atomic destruction.

The classical view of man tended to be a somber and pessimistic one, the feeling being that man had departed from a golden age and that human affairs were probably getting steadily worse. To be sure, there might be a return to some future golden age, but that prospect was not likely to be reached for several millenia. On the other hand, the romantic view of man which arose in the eighteenth and nineteenth centuries tended to regard him as basically good; evil was rather to be found in the corrupt institutions of society. If man were only allowed to return to some state of nature, he would find that such a natural state was good, kind and peaceful. The Marxists are prone to find evil in the bourgeois institutions of capitalism rather than in any basic fundamental disorder in man's heart.

Christianity takes both an optimistic and a pessimistic view of man. It has always regarded man as created in the image of God, and man's proper destiny as one of everlasting beatitude with God. But man is also a sinner, and unless he repents from his sin, he can only expect condemnation from God's justice. Yet, because of some primordial catastrophe which has somehow contaminated the human race, man needs help to counterbalance a natural inclination which he has toward sin and evil. C. S. Lewis wishes to explain all this to modern man not by departing from the doctrine of traditional Christianity, but by re-interpreting it and dressing it in a literary form appealing to twentieth-century moderns.

As one might expect, the first treatment of this subject occurs in *The Pilgrim's Regress*. The account of man's fall is told to John, the Everyman, by Mother Kirk. She says that when the Landlord decided to lease the country out, he chose as his first tenants a young married couple. He built a farm for them in the center of the land, where the soil was of the highest quality and the air the purest. They were to work the farm and keep the rest of the land as a park until it came time to divide it up among their heirs. The original lease was in perpetuity on the side of the Landlord, but the tenants could leave when they chose and come to live with the Landlord in the mountains. The only stipulation was that one of their sons stay on the farm and care for it.

Now there was a great mountain-apple tree growing in the center of the farm, but the Landlord had to warn his tenants that the fruit from it was most unsuitable for them. For a while the young man and his wife behaved very well. But somehow the wife made a new acquaintance, a landowner himself who had been born in the mountains. He was, in fact, one of the Landlord's own children, but he had quarreled with his Father and set up on his own. He had been a great land-grabber and presently had several tenants, though they were unaware of his identity. (John expresses surprise at this, but Mother Kirk replies, "That is how business is managed. The little people do not know the big people to whom they belong. The big people do not intend that they should.")

The enemy got to know the farmer's wife (Mother Kirk continues) and soon he persuaded her that the one thing she needed was a nice mountain-apple. She took one and ate it; then she talked the farmer into trying one. The moment he put out his hand and plucked the fruit, there was an earthquake. The country cracked open from north to south, and ever since, instead of the farm, there has been a gorge which the country people call the Grand Canyon. "But in my language its name is *Peccatum Adae*."[1]

C. S. Lewis calls this account of the temptation and Fall a "likely story" or "an old wives' tale." It is a myth, understanding by myth an account which contains truth, even though that truth may not be verifiable by historical means. But this is not to say that it may not be history. The emphasis is placed on the religious truth that is being taught; one prescinds from the questions whether or not it actually took place in history. It may have, it may not; the point is that the story embodies (much in the Platonic sense) a universal truth, a plausible account of something that may or may not have happened.

The results of this first disobedience were cataclysmic. The human spirit was no longer in full control of the human organism. The organs were no longer subjected to man's will, but fell under the rule of ordinary biochemical laws. Desires could no longer be controlled; the mind obeyed laws of psychological association and the like, and the will became caught in the tidal wave of mere nature. What man lost by the Fall, Lewis says, was his original specific nature. Man became his own idol; our present condition is explained by the fact that we are members of a spoiled species.

Are we personally responsible for this situation or not? We have all sinned "in" Adam by being mysteriously present in some manner or other. Adam is the head of the human race, and as long as we are members of the human race, we are children of Adam. In some sense, says Lewis, we share this guilt. This is more than a legal fiction, it is an actuality whose mystery may be impossible to penetrate. Lewis admits that his explanation of the Fall makes no pretense at profundity. For instance, he believes that the tree of life and the tree of the knowledge of good and evil symbolize some profound mystery, but he cannot say what. Nor does he wish to enter the controversy between Pelagius and Augustine with regard to the initiative in repentance and conversion—whether it comes from man or from God.

It is important to note that Lewis is skeptical about the so-called claims of anthropology. The evidence is too scant, he insists, to prove from a few selected artifacts what the religious nature of man was like centuries ago. He argues that there may have been men-like creatures capable of doing a number of things, but who were not yet men in the full sense of the word. He seems to leave the door open for the possibility that there were several such primordial figures who fell at the same time by an act or series of acts resulting in disobedience. And again, although he believes that this "likely story" lies outside of history and is best explained as a myth, he does not rule out the possibility that this primal disobedience actually did take place in history. I want to stress this because, while the balance of modern opinion favors the former theory (that the Fall is not an historical event), I personally can see no reason why the Fall may not have actually taken place *in* history. This is a less favored opinion, I realize, but it is nonetheless both possible and valid.

Lewis is careful to point out that the doctrine of the Fall excludes the idea that God is responsible for both good and evil (that it is he who created the present situation) as well as the notion that there is an evil principle which is eternally in conflict with a good principle. Zoroastrian dualism is thus excluded as a possible explanation.

Nor is Lewis unaware of the Satanic fall, for in *The Pilgrim's Regress* he alludes briefly to the land-grabber who had a quarrel with his Father and decided to set up on his own. This idea is not elaborated here, but it does receive more attention in *The Screwtape Letters* (XIX): "When the creation of man was first mooted and when, even at that stage, the Enemy freely confessed that he foresaw a certain episode about a cross, Our Father very naturally sought an interview and asked for an explanation. The Enemy gave no reply except to produce the cock-and-bull story about disinterested Love which He has been circulating ever since. This Our Father naturally could not accept. He implored the Enemy to lay His cards on the table, and gave Him every opportunity. He admitted that he felt a real anxiety to know the secret; the Enemy replied 'I wish with all my heart that you did.' It was, I imagine, at this stage in the interview that Our Father's disgust at such an unprovoked lack of confidence caused him to remove himself an infinite distance from the Presence with a suddenness which has given rise to the ridiculous enemy story that he was forcibly thrown out of Heaven."[2]

Here Lewis is following the traditional view that Satan was unwilling to accept the possibility of a future incarnation and felt that rather than continuing to serve in heaven, it would be better to reign in hell. In the *Preface to Paradise Lost*, Lewis summarizes the Augustinian doctrine of the Fall and points out that central to all sin is the fact of pride. Satan desired to "be like God," but through his own power rather than through participation in the Divine Being. This *I* which is at the center of all pride is an impossibility and therefore a lie, as Saint Thomas himself teaches.[3]

Lewis reiterates this theme in *Mere Christianity*. "How did the Dark Power go wrong?" he asks. "Here, no doubt, we ask a question to which human beings cannot give an answer with any certainty. A reasonable (and traditional) guess, based on our own experiences of going wrong, can, however, be offered. The moment you have a self at all, there is a possibility of putting yourself first —wanting to be the centre—wanting to be God, in fact. That was the sin of Satan: and that was the sin he taught the human race. . . . What Satan put into the heads of our remote ancestors was the idea that they could 'be like gods'—could set up on their own as if they had created themselves—be their own masters—invent some sort of happiness for themselves outside God, apart from God. And out of that hopeless attempt has come nearly all that we call human history—money, poverty, ambition, war, prostitution, classes, empires, slavery—the long terrible story of man trying to find something other than God which will make him happy."[4]

Although the devil features prominently in a number of Lewis's writings, he warns that we should not take Satan with the wrong kind of seriousness. The best antidote to temptation may be laughter, and we must remember that the devil cannot stand being mocked. Even though he has an intellect superior to any on earth, he only uses his intellect for nefarious ends, and when not engaged in temptation, the devil is an ass. There is a fascinating and horrifying scene in *Perelandra* where Ransom discovers the Un-Man as little more than a slobbering imbecile, a drooling idiot more pathetic than terrible. In *The Screwtape Letters*, Wormwood is warned about letting "the patient" know of the devils' existence. True, this forfeits some of the delights of terrorism that could be used in previous centuries, but it has its advantages in the skeptical twentieth century. This may have been so in the forties when Lewis was writing, but the recent spate of supernatural horror movies of one sort or another have rendered Lewis a bit out of date on this point.

We saw in Chapter 3 that the temptation theme undergirds the basic plot of *Perelandra. The Lion, the Witch and the Wardrobe* (the first Narnian chronicle) is another temptation story. Narnia has come under the grip of the devil. In this case it is the evil White Witch, who makes it "always winter and never Christmas." An ancient prophecy has declared that when four children sit on the four thrones of Cair Paravel, the White Witch's rule will have come to an end. Hearing that four children have recently entered Narnia, she sets out to prevent the prophecy's fulfillment by attempting to lure Edmund away from the other three. She fills him up with Turkish Delight and promises that some day he will rule as king. She is successful in her temptation, and Edmund's betrayal almost prevents the fulfillment of the prophecy. The witch can only be thwarted by Aslan's ultimate sacrifice of himself.

The ruin of Edmund is due to his particular passion for Turkish Delight. The candy means nothing to the witch; it is only a tool for the enslavement of the boy. The moral, of course, is that all created things are indeed essentially good, but evil arises from their abuse or misuse. The time-honored rule here is *tantum quantum*, using things only insofar as they will aid us in achieving the beatific vision. Edmund's inordinate attachment to one thing brought about his ruin.

The psychology of temptation is treated again in *The Silver Chair*, the fourth Narnian chronicle. Jill, Eustace and their guide, Puddleglum the Marsh-wiggle, have arrived in Underland in their search for Prince Rilian. The prince is rightful heir to the throne of Narnia, but he has been imprisoned and enchanted by a witch, the Queen of Underland. With the help of Aslan's fourth sign, the prince has been freed from his spell, but all are still captives of the witch. She attempts to persuade her prisoners that their quest is useless because hers is the only world; all other worlds, particularly Overland (Narnia), are merely illusions. The prisoners are unable to prove by reasoning or logic that there is any other world than the one they are in, so the witch taunts them with these words:

"I see that we should do no better with your *lion* [Aslan], as you call it, than we did with your *sun*. You have seen lamps, and so you imagined a bigger and better lamp and called it the *sun*. You've seen cats, and now you want a bigger and better cat, and it's to be called a *lion*. Well, 'tis a pretty make-believe, though, to say the truth, it would suit you all better if you were younger. And look how you can put nothing into your make-believe without copying it from the real world, this world of mine, which is the only world. But even you children are too old for such play. As for you, my lord Prince, that art a man full grown, fie upon you! Are you not ashamed of such toys? Come, all of you. Put away these childish tricks. I have work for you all in the real world. There is no Narnia, no Overworld, no sky, no sun, no Aslan."[5]

With the help of a fire which has been heavily incensed and the steady thrum, thrum, thrum of her musical instrument, the witch is almost successful in her "destruction of faith." The humans begin to assent to this abjuration, when suddenly Puddleglum breaks the spell:

"Suppose we *have* only dreamed, or made up, all those things—trees and grass and sun and moon and stars and Aslan himself. Suppose we have. Then all I can say is that, in that case, the made-up things seem a good deal more important than the real ones. Suppose this black pit of a kingdom of yours *is* the only world. Well, it strikes me as a pretty poor one. And that's a funny thing, when you come to think of it. We're just babies making up a game, if you're right. But four babies playing a game can make a play-world which licks your real world hollow. That's why I'm going to stand by the play world. I'm on Aslan's side even if there isn't any Aslan to lead it. I'm going to live as like a Narnian as I can even if there isn't any Narnia."[6]

This almost sounds like Death-of-God theology or even Christless Christianity. But it is meant to be just the opposite: a ringing affirmation that has the effect of destroying the power of the witch completely. What Lewis is saying is that subjective feelings of God, freedom and immortality are valid because they have been put there by an objective reality. Puddleglum, of course, believes this; he is postulating a situation which is only hypothetical at best, nor does Lewis wish to imply that his hypothesis is necessarily valid. The significance of this passage from *The Silver Chair* lies more in the strategy of the witch, which can be compared somewhat to that of Screwtape.

Although it stands sixth in *The Chronicles of Narnia, The Magician's Nephew* stands chronologically first because it relates how Aslan created Narnia and gave the gift of speech to its animals. At the same time, its main character, Digory (the Magician's nephew), undergoes a moral testing and direct confrontation with evil, again in the person of the witch, here called Jadis. After creating Narnia, Aslan sadly announces that an evil has already entered the world; but for the time being Narnia will be safe, thanks to certain supernatural protections which will, however, not be permanent. Aslan sends Digory, accompanied by his friend Polly, on a quest for a silver apple which can be planted in Narnia and by its fragrance ward off evil.

Digory's winged horse, Fledge, flies them to the garden and Digory enters it alone. No sooner is he inside than he discovers that the witch has climbed over the wall and is present in the garden also. Digory plucks the apple and is about to flee when the witch stops him and commences her enticement:

> "You have plucked fruit in the garden yonder. You have it in your pocket now. And you are going to carry it back, untasted, to the Lion; for *him* to eat, for *him* to use. You simpleton! Do you know what that fruit is? I will tell you. It is the apple of youth, the apple of life. I know, for I have tasted it; and I feel already such changes in myself that I know I shall never grow old or die. Eat it, Boy, eat it; and you and I will both live forever and be king and queen of this whole world —or of your world if we decide to go back there."[7]

This tactic fails, so the witch attacks Digory at his most sensitive spot, his sick mother. The witch exclaims:

> "Do you not see, Fool, that one bite of that apple would heal her? You have it in your pocket. We are here by ourselves and the Lion is far away. Use your Magic and go back to your own world. A min-

ute later you can be at your Mother's bedside, giving her the fruit. Five minutes later you will see the colour coming back to her face. She will tell you the pain is gone. Soon she will tell you she feels stronger. Then she will fall asleep—think of that; hours of sweet natural sleep, without pain, without drugs. Next day everyone will be saying how wonderfully she has recovered. Soon she will be quite well again."[8]

The witch continues to press her advantage:

"What has Lion ever done for you that you should be his slave?" said the Witch. "What can he do to you once you are back in your own world? And what would your Mother think if she knew that you *could* have taken her pain away and given her back her life and saved your Father's heart from being broken, and that you *wouldn't*—that you'd rather run messages for a wild animal in a strange world that is no business of yours?"[9]

Digory blurts out that his mother would not approve of either stealing or not keeping promises. The witch counters with:

"But she need never know. . . . You wouldn't tell her how you'd got the apple. Your Father need never know. No one in your world need know anything about this whole story. You needn't take the little girl back with you, you know."[10]

The last remark was a fatal mistake for the witch, because it exposed her whole hand and showed Digory what a selfish person she was. *He* would never have left Polly behind. What Lewis wants to show is that satanic temptations can be self-defeating in the end. The devil pushes his advantage too far; he oversteps his mark, and that is why the devil is an ass.

The temptation resisted, Digory and Polly fly back to Aslan, and in a magnificent line which concludes the chapter Digory says to the lion, "I've brought you the apple you wanted, sir."[11] It is not a triumphant line. In fact, Digory is not sure whether he has acted correctly or not; he only knows that he has obeyed orders as best he was able. Later he is rewarded, not merely by the approval of the lion, but by the gift of a silver apple from the newly-planted tree in Narnia. And when Digory's mother finally eats the apple, she undergoes a remarkable improvement. As in *Perelandra* and *The Silver Chair*, the temptation story has a "happy ending."

In worlds where no Fall has occurred, it is difficult, if not impossible, to convey the meaning of evil. In *The Magician's Nephew*, when Aslan makes his announcement that an evil has entered the world, the astonished talking animals ask, "*What* did he say had entered the world?—a Neevil—What's a Neevil?—No, he didn't say a Neevil, he said a weevil—Well, what's that?"[12] And in the space trilogy Ransom has difficulty explaining the concept of evil to one of the rational beings on Malacandra. He finally hits on the idea of bentness. The silent planet (earth) has become very bent; the people there are held prey by a bent Oyarsa who rules from his own world (hell).

This is an interesting explanation of the meaning of evil, one which Lewis may have taken from Pseudo-Dionysius. It is a felicitous choice for at least two reasons: something that is bent out of shape is obviously distorted, is not normal, does not conform to the usual pattern, represents a lack in some object (person, relationship) of a quality that should be present; by the same token, the bentness is also a nothingness. It never exists by itself; it can only exist in something good. It is a nothing, a lack rather than a something. Hence, nothing is totally evil, since evil can only exist in a good. The devil is not totally evil inasmuch as he is a being, and every being by the fact that it exists is good. *Omne ens est bonum*, as the philosopher says.

This idea, however, is more compelling logically than psychologically. We somehow feel that evil is more than lack, distortion, bentness, nothing. For all of its non-being, it can sometimes feel very effective. And it is difficult to think of some of Lewis's fictional characters as merely bent. The witches in *The Chronicles of Narnia* are malevolent figures seeking to work positive harm. So is Screwtape, and so are Frost, Winter and Fairy Hardcastle in *That*

Hideous Strength. Thus for Lewis to say that evil is merely a privation of good is not altogether convincing in the face of some of the evil he has depicted for us.

White states that Lewis held no optimistic view of the essential goodness of human nature.[13] It would be better to say that while he did believe in the essential goodness of people, he was well aware of their potential for excessive evil. The temptations of Screwtape were subtle and not spectacular; the aim was to win souls. If the temptations succeeded, then the final end was the miserific vision, for the destiny of people was to be either an everlasting glory or an everlasting horror. But Lewis also has a strong sense of cosmic evil. We wrestle, he would say, not (merely) against flesh and blood, but also against the powers of darkness. The struggle is both terrestrial and celestial.

Even though Lewis was disinterested in history—at least political history—he had a firm grip on the Christian view of the end of history. He could see that both wheat and tares grow together until the end of time, and at the end of the world there will be a sorting out of the good from the bad, the false from the true. The parables of the drag-net, the mustard seed, and the wheat and the tares were clear guidelines for Lewis in his understanding of the contest between good and evil and the culmination of history at the end of the world.

Jesus Christ and Redemption

It is apparent to everyone, Lewis says, that the universe is in disorder, and Christians believe that an evil power has somehow gotten control of things. Of course, this raises problems. If God is omnipotent, why does he allow this state of affairs, and if he is not, how can we believe in a good God? The answer is that the present situation is and is not the will of God. As long as people have the power of choice, this means that they can choose bad things as well as good; otherwise their free will would be only seeming free choice. To illustrate this, Lewis gives the example of a mother who tells her children that they must tidy up the school-room on their own each night, and then one night goes upstairs to find it in total disarray. This is clearly against her will, yet it was her will that gave the children the power to keep things straight or not, and it has been her will that they exercise their own free power of choice.[1]

As for the evil power, Christians believe that Satan rebelled against God by wanting to put himself first, and that he has taught a good part of the human race to put itself first and God last. It is this self-centeredness which makes civilizations rise and fall, or individual lives founder on the rocks of selfishness. "Terrific energy is expended—civilizations are built up—excellent institutions devised; but each time something goes wrong. Some fatal flaw always brings the selfish and cruel people to the top and it all slides back into misery and ruin. In fact, the machine conks. It seems to start up all right and runs a few yards, and then it breaks down. They are trying to run it on the wrong juice. That is what Satan has done to us humans."[2]

If free will makes evil possible, why does God allow a situation of this sort? Lewis answers that free will also makes possible the only goodness, joy and love worth having. It is a calculated risk which God apparently thinks is worth the taking. Otherwise we would be in a universe of machines, of automata, of robots. "The happiness which God designs for His higher creatures is the happiness of being freely, voluntarily united to Him and to each other in an ecstasy of love and delight compared with which the most rapturous love between a man and woman on this earth is mere milk and water. And for that they must be free."[3]

There are some who may disagree with God and maintain that the misuse of free will is so great that it would have been better if God had avoided this universal calamity entirely, but in arguing against God (Lewis reminds us) we are arguing against the power that gives us the ability to argue at all. Lewis is not altogether convincing on this point. It would be better to say that from God's vantage point things no doubt look much different than from our own, so that we should acquiesce in the given situation as we find it. In any case, to those who would ask why God made us of such rotten stuff that we went wrong, Lewis would reply that we are made of very good stuff. "The better stuff a creature is made of— the cleverer and stronger and freer it is—then the better it will be if it goes right, but also the worse it will be if it goes wrong. A cow cannot be very good or very bad; a dog can be both better and worse; a child better and worse still; an ordinary man still more so; a man of genius still more so; a superhuman spirit best—or worst—of all."[4]

And, Lewis points out, God has not left the universe to run entirely by itself. The evil power has not been able to take over completely because God has given us weapons to resist it. For one thing, he has given to each person a conscience and the ability to determine right from wrong. It is a matter of record that not a few people have tried very hard to obey the dictates of conscience. God has also sent the human race "good dreams," by which Lewis means that much of Christianity was foreshadowed in the pagan religions, and most especially in the theme of the dying and rising god who bestows benefits on mankind. This is a most important theme in Lewis, but we can only touch on it briefly here. The religions which preceded Christianity were not inventions of the demons, but rather adumbrations of what would some day actually occur in the history of mankind. I call this the benign interpretation of the nature and mystery religions (Saint Clement of Alexandria) rather than the harsh notion of Tertullian that these primitive cults were merely meant to lead men astray.

A third thing God did was to choose the Jews as a special race who would uphold his monotheism and combine this with ethical behavior. That is what the Old Testament is all about, and indeed that was the whole purpose of Jewish history from the time of Abraham until the time of Christ. But the real shock occurs when a Jew appears who claims also to be God.

It is not quite correct to say that Lewis pays little attention to the earthly life of Jesus, but it is true that what Lewis emphasizes is the person and work of Christ, and perhaps in this he is like Saint Paul. But when we have a person who suddenly appears somewhat mysteriously and claims always to have existed, who claims to forgive sins, and who says that he is going to come to judge the world at the end of time, one may wonder why the crucifixion did not occur even sooner than it did. If we remember that the Jews were not pantheists, that their God was Being Itself, who existed outside of time, what Jesus claimed for himself was very shocking, "quite simply, the most shocking thing that has ever been uttered by human lips."[5]

Lewis makes a good deal of the fact that Jesus claimed to forgive sins. The presumption involved here is enormous. Here is a man who seems to forgive you for your sins without consulting the people who were directly injured by your sins. He acts as though he were the person who had been offended! "Asinine fatuity" is the label which charitably would be put on such conduct. In fact, it would be both presumptuous and silly, if Jesus were not actually God. And that is no doubt why the charge of blasphemy was frequently levelled against him.[6] Lewis sums up the argument in a paragraph which is one of the most brilliant in all of his writings:

> I am trying here to prevent anyone saying the really foolish thing that people often say about Him: 'I'm ready to accept Jesus as a great moral teacher, but I don't accept His claim to be God.' That is the one thing we must not say. A man who was merely a man and said the sort of things Jesus said would not be a great moral teacher. He would either be a lunatic—on a level with the man who says he is a poached egg—or else he would be the Devil of Hell. You must make your choice. Either this man was, and is, the Son of God; or else a madman or something worse. You can shut Him up for a fool, you can spit at Him and kill Him as a demon; or you can fall at His feet and call Him Lord and God. But let us not come with any patronising nonsense about His being a great human teacher. He has not left that open to us. He did not intend to.[7]

This is not to say that Jesus did not give a good deal of moral teaching. But that was not the main purpose of his ministry. The world had seen other moral teachers aplenty and had paid them little heed. The chief purpose of Jesus' ministry was to suffer and to die, and afterwards to rise again. The New Testament is quite

clear on that, and so is the witness of the early Church. In some
manner, the death and resurrection of Christ has reconciled mankind to God. We do not know how this has happened; we only
know *that* it has happened, and the fact that it has happened is far
more important than any theories of how it has happened. You
can say that Christ's death broke the power of demons. You can
say that Christ has ransomed us from sin. You can say that the
mercy of God has satisfied the justice of God. The Church has
never put its official seal of approval on any one of these theories.
Lewis is not concerned with theories; he wants us to get hold of
the central fact that Christ's death has somehow put us right with
God and given us a fresh start.

When people are hungry or tired, they eat dinner and then feel
better. Long before the theory of vitamins was discovered or the
science of dietetics developed, people knew that eating could give
them added strength. But very few people ever bother to find out
how the process of digestion works; for most people it really isn't
important. The "formula" for knowing *that* something is true
must not be confused with the mental picture or diagram of why
or *how* something works. In modern astronomy, this is especially
true; the universe is more like a great thought than a biological
organism, and more like an organism than the eighteenth century
concept of the universe as a great machine. Reality today is often
best expressed by mathematical equations.

Theories of the Atonement are to be avoided like the plague.
We should never think of the Atonement as a kind of transaction
that has involved God's paying some sort of ransom to the devil.
The only theory that Lewis offers is the idea of man's indebtedness
("being in a hole") because of sin, an indebtedness which Christ
has satisfied for each one of us. God has let us off in this sense:
that what we could not pay for ourselves, Christ has paid for us—
thus wiping the slate clean. The point is that every man is a rebel

before God; what he needs is not some recipe for moral improvement, he needs to make a self-surrender, to lay down his arms, to admit that he has all along been on the wrong track, to say he's sorry. In a word, what is called for is *repentance*.

The New Testament term for repentance is *metanoia*—change of mind or change of heart. It is not a single act, but an ongoing process. It occurs not once, but every day. It is more than just "eating humble pie," it involves an entire reformation of character. It is a willing humiliation and a kind of death; it is the process by which God takes over your life. But here we need help to do something which God in his nature never does at all: to surrender, to suffer, to submit, to die; and since God can only share what he has (and these things he does not have) how can he be of any help to us?

Lewis falls back on the Incarnation. If God becomes man, he can help us because he can then, as man, surrender his will and suffer and die, and he can do all of this perfectly because he is God. Thus the God-man becomes the perfect penitent by amalgamating our human nature into one Person. Fortunately Lewis does not speak of the amalgamation of Christ's human nature with his divine nature, and thus the Chalcedonian formula is left intact. Our attempts at dying "will succeed only if we men share in God's dying, just as our thinking can succeed only because it is a drop out of the ocean of His intelligence: but we cannot share God's dying unless God dies; and He cannot die except by being a man. That is the sense in which He pays our debt, and suffers for us what He Himself need not suffer at all."[8]

"The perfect surrender and humiliation were undergone by Chirst: perfect because He was God, surrender and humiliation because He was man."[9] Now, by copying Christ, by putting on Christ, the Christian somehow participates in the Christ-life of perfect surrender to God. Christ is in us, but we are also in Christ.

The Christ-life goes on inside of us, nourishing, protecting, growing, sometimes calling us to repentance, even to "begin over
again." It continues until the day of our death. The imitation of
Christ involves the kind of voluntary death which Christ himself
carried out.

Three vehicles are necessary to foster this Christ-life within us:
belief, Baptism and Holy Communion. Lewis says very little about
any of the three. By belief, he means not only an acceptance of the
basic, traditional truths of Christianity (faith in the intellectual
sense) but also implicit trust in God's leading us along the path
chosen for us. This is a more Protestant interpretation of faith; it
is addressed primarily to the will. Of Baptism, Lewis merely notes
its necessity, which he finds clearly stated in the New Testament.
Nor does he give any precise interpretation of Holy Communion.
He simply indicates its necessity as well. That is as far as he wishes
to go in *Mere Christianity*, because he realizes well that this is a
controverted question. Since he himself was a High Anglican (he
disavowed the *High* part, but he was one nevertheless), he believed in the real presence of Christ in the Eucharist. But it is also
fair to say that he apparently did not think this terribly important.
He rarely uses the word *Mass*, again because of its controversial
interpretation. To avoid that which divides Christians, Lewis does
not develop a coherent sacramental doctrine.

The sanctification of a person involves both body and soul, both
matter and spirit. Matter is a creation of God, and therefore not
intrinsically evil. And since we are not meant to be purely spiritual
beings, God chooses to sanctify us through bread and wine, oil and
water. Christianity is after all a materialistic religion; even the
Second Member of the Blessed Trinity became incarnate.

What is the purpose of all this? Why does God delay his coming? Why does he not land and invade in full force? Is it that he
is not strong enough? Lewis concludes "What Christians Believe"

(the second section of *Mere Christianity*) with the following observation:

> [God] wants to give us the chance of joining His side freely. I do not suppose you and I would have thought much of a Frenchman who waited till the Allies were marching into Germany and then announced he was on our side. God will invade. But I wonder whether people who ask God to interfere openly and directly in our world quite realise what it will be like when He does. When that happens, it is the end of the world. When the author walks on to the stage the play is over. God is going to invade, all right: but what is the good of saying you are on His side then, when you see the whole natural universe melting away like a dream and something else—something it never entered your head to conceive—comes crashing in; something so beautiful to some of us and so terrible to others that none of us will have any choice left? For this time it will be God without disguise; something so overwhelming that it will strike either irresistible love or irresistible horror into every creature. It will be too late then to choose your side.[10]

These ideas are recapitulated and developed further in "Beyond Personality." The Son of God became a man to enable men to become sons of God. This means that the Second Person of the Trinity was born into the world (after spending nine months in his mother's womb) as a man, and chose an earthly career which involved mortifying his earthly desires. He accepted poverty, misunderstanding, betrayal by a close friend, ridicule, physical abuse and an execution by torture. After thus being killed (every day in a sense), the human creature (united to the Divine Son) came to life again. For the first time in its history, the world saw a real man.

But in God's eyes, the human race is a single entity because everyone in it is somehow related to everybody else. Hence the death and resurrection of Christ have affected all of humanity in a new way. Humanity has passed from temporary biological life (bíos) into timeless spiritual life (zoé) and can thus be said to be saved already in principle. To be sure, each individual must appropriate this new kind of spiritual life for himself, but the really tough part has been done for us, the part which none of us could have done for ourselves. One of our race already has this new life; if we get close to him, we can catch some of this new life by close association. Lewis calls this "good infection." The person and work of Christ can then be summarized in the following manner:

> You can say that Christ died for our sins. You may say that the Father has forgiven us because Christ has done for us what we ought to have done. You may say that we are washed in the blood of the Lamb. You may say that Christ has defeated death. They are all true. If any of them do not appeal to you, leave it alone and get on with the formula that does. And, whatever you do, do not start quarrelling with other people because they use a different formula from yours.[11]

Although it is not entirely satisfactory, Lewis uses the analogy of toy soldiers or tin soldiers that are being brought to life. The analogy is inadequate because what happens to one toy tin soldier does not necessarily affect any of the other tin soldiers, whereas the person and work of Christ have affected the entire human race. What has been effected in the objective order must now be applied in the subjective order. Humans, however, are obstinate. They do not wish to be transformed; they think you are killing them. They will do everything they can to prevent you. They want to hold on to their natural life (their bíos) even though they are destined to enjoy supernatural life (zoé). This is, of course, what the Christian Gospel is all about.

One of Lewis's favorite themes is that the satanic strategy is often to frighten people with one error, in the hope that they will fall into the opposite error. Two such opposite errors are extreme individualism versus totalitarianism. The fact that Christ has altered the entire human race does not mean that individuals are not important. Tom, Dick and Harry are different from one another and must be treated as separate cases. They may all be part of humanity, but they cannot be merged with humanity indiscriminately. It is a paradox of Christianity that Christ died for each single individual. In *The Lion, the Witch and the Wardrobe*, Aslan died only for the boy Edmund. Similarly, the passion of Christ must be understood as applying to the single individual. It would be quite false to infer that the extreme suffering of the Passion was due to the large number of people who needed saving. It would have been just the same even if only one individual had been involved.

A somewhat abstruse point on which Lewis falters is the question of why God the Father did not beget many Sons, instead of creating "toy soldiers" and having them brought to life in such a difficult and painful way. It is purely theoretical, and Lewis urges that when we ask what God might have done, we enter the realm of unreality. Also, if there were more than one Son of God, Lewis says, they would have to be different from one another, yet all related to the Father and to one another in the same way. That is unimaginable unless we haul in the concepts of space and time, which themselves are created things. It would be better if Lewis had simply replied that the Son is the image of the Father; there can actually be only one Logos since that involves the Father in his totality, and such an intellectual generation must be only one single undivided entity. But the theoretical question is of little moment and should not detain us here.

In order that Christ may work effectively in the hearts of each person endowed with zoé, a certain "amount of pretense" is necessary. We must put on Christ by dressing up as Christ. Since he himself has commanded this, the point is that by dressing up as Christ, or pretending Christ, we become more like Christ. Men become mirrors; they become carriers of Christ to other men. This theme runs through a number of Lewis's writings.

But this cannot be done without the aid of Christ himself. He can do it because he is the Son of his Father (divine), but also because he is the Son of Man (human). By imparting his zoé to his followers, he makes them become more and more like himself. And it is a cooperative work. Christ works within us, but we also work. The enterprise has to be attributed to both operators. In this way Lewis sidesteps the sticky problem of grace and free will, and the celebrated argument between the Dominicans and the Jesuits in the seventeenth century over the *De Auxiliis* question.

Christianity is not primarily concerned with keeping a set of rules. It is, rather, a question of coming into contact with a Person. It is like painting a portrait. The Christian life is both easy and difficult. We are not doing it on our own; we have support. Each time we fall, God will pick us up again. On the other hand, we are striving for absolute perfection. That is what God wants for us. We are to model ourselves after a Person, and our choices become concerned not so much with good and evil, but with good and better. More and more areas of the personal life must be surrendered to the God-Man. Borrowing an illustration from George MacDonald, the nineteenth century Scottish novelist, Lewis writes:

> Imagine yourself as a living house. God comes in to rebuild that house. At first, perhaps, you can understand what He is doing. He is getting the drains right and stopping the leaks in the roof and so on: you knew that those jobs needed doing and so you are not surprised. But presently he starts knocking the house about in a way that hurts abominably and does not seem to make sense. What on earth is He up to? The explanation is that He is building quite a different house from the one you thought of—throwing out a new wing here, putting on an extra floor there, running up towers, making courtyards. You thought you were going to be made into a decent little cottage: but He is building a palace. He intends to come and live in it Himself.[12]

The sanctification of the person is the sole purpose of the Gospel. All else must point to this, be it church, liturgy, worship, social service or ethics. And when enough persons have caught this "good infection," we may see some surprising things; we may even see Nature herself begin to be straightened out, as she waits for the redemption of the sons of God. For these new people will populate a new universe. The bad dream will be over and it will be morning.

However, the call to perfection also involves counting the cost. Christ does not tinker with lives, nor merely patch them up, he produces a new man destined for perfection. The only power in the universe which can keep one from reaching this goal is one's self. The challenge is to work toward the goal step by step. God is easy to please, but hard to satisfy. Yet the divine intention is not to make us into merely nice people, but new men. That is the reason that God made us in the first place.

This opposition between "nice people" and "new men" comes out in *That Hideous Strength*. The National Institute of Coordinated Experiments, whose aim is to produce a new type of man by sterilization of the unfit, liquidation of backward races, selective breeding, biochemical conditioning and direct manipulation of the brain, can also be abbreviated with the letters N.I.C.E. But like the Pharisees of old, these scientific people are once-born men, and their aim is to capture and exploit the universe for themselves. "Nice people" are still unregenerated, self-centered people.[18]

But if Christianity is really true, it must follow that all Christians are "nicer" than all non-Christians. Yet Miss Bates who claims to be a Christian is a nasty-tempered old maid, while Dick who is not a Christian has a genial personality, is a wonderful person to be with, is a very pleasant pagan! Lewis rightly warns that such comparisons can be quite false. Everything we have, including our good health, our sunny dispositions and our pleasant natures are a gift from God. What do we have that we have not received? The proper question to ask is, What would Dick be like if he *were* a Christian, and what would Miss Bates be like if she were *not* a Christian?

The world is not fair and God is not democratic. Some people possess ten talents and others only one. God is well aware that some people are trying to operate with old, worn-out machinery. Someday he will replace it, but in the meantime the Christian life involves doing the best you can with what you have. As a matter of fact, the less-advantaged people may be better off. In his usual pungent style, Lewis says:

> But if you are a poor creature—poisoned by a wretched upbringing in some house full of vulgar jealousies and senseless quarrels—saddled, by no choice of your own, with some loathsome sexual perversion— nagged day in and day out by an inferiority complex that makes you snap at your best friends—do not despair. He knows all about it. You are one of the poor whom He blessed. He knows what a wretched machine you are trying to drive. Keep on. Do what you can. One day (perhaps in another world, but perhaps far sooner than that) he will fling it on the scrap-heap and give you a new one. And then you may astonish us all—not least yourself: for you have learned your driving in a hard school. (Some of the last will be first and some of the first will be last.)[14]

Therefore it is *transformation*, not mere self-improvement, which lies at the heart of Christianity. In fact, it is the *new men* who are the key to the evolutionary process, who are setting it off in a direction which formerly would have been unthinkable. In a way reminiscent of some of Teilhard de Chardin's writing, Lewis insists both in *The Problem of Pain* and in "Beyond Personality" (*Mere Christianity*) that a new "twist" in evolution has already occurred. It began in Palestine two thousand years ago. It differs from the previous steps in "evolution" because it comes from outside nature, and also because (1) sex is not involved; (2) it depends in large part on man's choice, his free will; (3) Christ is not only the first instance of this new evolutionary process, He *is* the process because He brings the zoé, the new life, thus imparting "good infection"; (4) the step is an accelerated one occurring in a relatively short period of time (two thousand years is nothing in the history of the universe); and (5) the stakes are high because of the risk involved to each individual—his own personal salvation or damnation.[15]

Fortunately, babies do not have the choice of whether they will be born or not. If they did, they might prefer the warmth and security of their mothers' wombs and refuse to enter the cold, cruel world. But that way lies death. Every individual now has the power of personal choice to determine whether he or she desires to be part of the new ongoing evolutionary process. The Person and work of Christ have made this possible in the objective order. It must now be applied subjectively. Near the end of "Beyond Personality," Lewis makes a sort of "altar-call" appeal, and it is an excellent quotation with which to conclude this chapter on Redemption.

> What can you ever really know of other people's souls—of their temptations, their opportunities, their struggles? One soul in the whole creation you do know: and it is the only one whose fate is placed in your hands. If there is a God, you are, in a sense, alone with Him. You cannot put Him off with speculations about your next door neighbours or memories of what you have read in books. What will all that chatter and hearsay count (will you even be able to remember it?) when the anaesthetic fog which we call "nature" or "the real world" fades away and the Presence in which you have always stood becomes palpable, immediate, and unavoidable?[16]

6

The Church and Sacraments

In this chapter we want to examine some of Lewis's ideas about the Church. Surely the doctrine of the Church is an important ingredient in understanding Christianity—at least Saint Paul thought so. What has Lewis to say? Actually, precious little. The main sources are two: some significant passages in *The Pilgrim's Regress*, which (be it noted) is an early work, and some references in *The Screwtape Letters*. Then there are some obiter dicta in letters to friends.

"Jargon, not argument, is your best ally in keeping him from the Church," says Screwtape to Wormwood in his very first communication regarding their "patient."[1] This is a short but important reference, because it indicates Lewis's belief that the Church is important to salvation, in fact may even be indispensable to the "patient's" salvation. The letter immediately following describes for us the Church as Screwtape views it. "The Church as we see her spread out through all time and space and rooted in eternity, terrible as an army with banners. That, I confess, is a spectacle which makes our boldest tempters uneasy. But fortunately it is quite invisible to these humans."[2]

With bold and convincing strokes, Lewis paints for us the

Church militant, suffering and triumphant. But he also confines this sketch to the Church invisible. The Church visible, Screwtape goes on to tell us, is apt to be a sham Gothic erection with worshippers like the oily grocer, who hands out a shabby little book containing corrupt texts of a number of religious lyrics, mostly bad, and in very small print.[3] No matter that these odd looking parishioners may indeed be members of the body of Christ, if their life style looks ridiculous, their religion must likewise be ridiculous. While Lewis is contrasting the actuality with the ideal, he is admitting the necessity for both. Or rather, he is arguing that corporate worship in a church, in *the* Church, is indispensable if the "patient" is to make progress in the Christian life.

The seventh Screwtape letter returns once again to the Church, this time in a discussion of factions. Screwtape says, "We want the Church to be small not only that fewer men may know the Enemy but also that those who do may acquire the uneasy intensity and the defensive self-righteousness of a secret society or clique. The Church herself is, of course, heavily defended, and we have never yet quite succeeded in giving her *all* the characteristics of a faction; but subordinate factions within her have often produced admirable results, from the parties of Paul and of Apollos at Corinth down to the High and Low parties in the Church of England."[4]

I infer that Lewis is in sympathy with Screwtape at this point: he believes that factions undermine the Church. But this may be to dismiss factions in a too cavalier manner. Factions occur when there are differences of opinion, varying theological beliefs and sometimes opposite goals. Lewis may deplore high and low parties in the Church of England, but it seems clear to this writer that he would have lost little time in coming down for the High Church position if he had been forced to make a choice. He certainly did not believe that all factions were equally in the right, but he did believe that they should try to live together if at all possible.

In *The Pilgrim's Regress*, there are two lengthy passages dealing with the Church. The first is in Book 5, chapter 1 when John, the pilgrim, and his companion, Vertue, encounter an old woman seated in a kind of rocking chair at the very edge of a precipice. " 'Oh, it's you, Mother Kirk, is it?' said Vertue, and added in an undertone to John, 'I have seen her about the cliffs more than once. Some of the country people say she is second-sighted, and some that she is crazy.' 'I shouldn't trust her,' said John in the same tone. 'She looks to me much more like a witch.' "[5]

This is a priceless description of the divine and human nature of the Church, along with its general characteristic of being a sign and contradiction in the world. Mother Kirk offers to carry John and Vertue down the Grand Canyon, but she looks inadequate to the task. She assures them, however, that the Landlord has given her the necessary power. In fact, she is his own daughter-in-law. John complains that the Landlord must be a strange one because he has made a road running up to the very edge of the precipice. Mother Kirk replies that the canyon is later than the road, which once ran all around the world, and she proceeds to tell the story of the Landlord, his tenants and the first transgression. She then says that the whole country is now more or less contaminated, with the result that one needs very complicated rules in order to stay healthy.[6]

Mother Kirk again offers to carry the two young men down the canyon. However, both John and Vertue have been self-sufficient up to this point, so they decline her aid and elect to explore some passage either to the north or to the south by themselves. They cannot accept the proposition that they must do exactly as Mother Kirk tells them. She sends them cheerily on their way with the veiled suggestion that she will meet them again.

In this incident it is clear that the Church is the custodian of the story about man's first disobedience and the forbidden fruit.

It is also clear that one needs her help in some way. Trusting in their own self-reliance, John and Vertue set off on a wild goose chase. They have decided that Mother Kirk is clearly insane, but the insanity is on their part for dismissing her as a crazy old woman. This portrait of Mother Kirk as a bumbling old crone is in marked contrast to the way she appears in the second meeting between her and the two travelers. This occurs in Book 9, chapter 4.

Previous to this encounter, John has been having tea with Mr. Broad (who represents a faction in the Church which Lewis does not like), to whom he addresses this question: "Supposing a man *did* have to cross the canyon. Is it true that he would have to rely on Mother Kirk?" Mr. Broad replies, "Ah Mother Kirk! I love and honour her from the bottom of my heart, but I trust that loving her does not mean being blind to her faults. We are none of us infallible. If I sometimes feel that I must differ from her at present, it is because I honour all the more the *idea* that she stands for, the thing she may yet become. For the moment, there is no denying that she has let herself get a little out of date."[7]

"I want my island," replies John, and the implication is that he will rely on Mother Kirk to get him there if that proves to be the only way. After a falling out with Vertue and some further encounters, John eventually meets Death in the darkness this side of the canyon. He has reached an impasse. Death orders him to jump or be thrown, give in or struggle. "I would sooner do the first, if I could," says John. "Then I am your servant and no more your master," Death replies. "The cure of death is dying. He who lays down his liberty in that act receives it back. Go down to Mother Kirk."[8]

On the floor of the canyon stands Mother Kirk, crowned and sceptered in the midst of a bright moonlit circle; not far from her sits Vertue. They are both on the edge of a large pool. John announces to the assembled group, "I have come to give myself up."

"It is well," says Mother Kirk. "You have come a long way round to reach this place, whither I would have carried you in a few moments. But it is very well."[9]

John is ordered to take off his filthy rags and dive into the pool; he must dive and not jump, for he is to travel to the other side through a tunnel that runs under the bottom of the pool. All the states of mind through which he has ever passed rise up to dissuade him from this act. But finally he follows Vertue's example, rubs his hands, shuts his eyes, despairs, and dives. He swims a long time under the water and then emerges on the other side among a host of people.

In this second encounter with Mother Kirk, Lewis wants us to understand that she is the custodian of the waters of Baptism. There is also a brief reference to the Eucharist, so the two major sacraments and Mother Kirk are linked together. The pilgrims whom John meets on the far side, and who are to accompany him at the beginning of his journey, are clearly children of Mother Kirk who each has his or her own road to travel. The only way John can reach his appointed destination is to turn about and travel the way he came. On the trip back, he meets some of the characters he had met before, but this time in a new guise. Viewed from the standpoint of the pilgrim, pride, ignorance and luxury appear now in quite different dress. Mother Kirk, however, does not reappear in the story.

From the foregoing, we can now summarize Lewis's doctrine of the Church. The Church is both new and old, spread out through space and time and rooted in eternity, but to mortal eyes it appears to be slightly ridiculous. Its members are the last people one wants to see or to have any dealings with. Its human element is much more apparent than its divine, and there is no mention of a pope at its head. In the conversation with Mr. Broad, where Mr. Broad denies that the Church is infallible, Lewis seems to be taking the opposite position: that the Church's teaching, at any rate, is infallible. But nowhere does he describe her as one, holy, catholic or apostolic.

Is membership in the Church necessary for salvation? Lewis would say yes; at least, no one can cross the canyon without the aid of Mother Kirk. Is she divine? Yes, Mother Kirk refers to herself as the Landlord's daughter-in-law, which seems conclusive evidence that Christ founded the Church and considers her also his bride. Must the Church have a hierarchical structure? Lewis is not a democrat with regard to church authority, and we can at least say indirectly yes to this question. Lewis numbered a good many priests among his friends, Dom Bede Griffiths for one, so he was undoubtedly on good terms with them.

The point at which Lewis is conspicuously lacking is with regard to the Petrine theory and the Bishop of Rome. Some have argued that he deliberately avoided this question as separating Protestants from Roman Catholics, and his aim is to present only that which is "mere" Christianity. But the more likely answer, in this writer's opinion, is that he did not really believe in it.

In fact, what Lewis is trying to do is that which Newman found ultimately impossible. Lewis is trying to shore up the old via media, with its avoidance of the subtractions of the sects and the additions of Rome. But what he considers peripheral is actually crucial to the entire structure. For what makes the Roman Catholic church unique is its living magisterium speaking authoritatively on matters of faith and morals. Lewis might well take advantageous refuge in a three-branch theory of the Church, but what he is not yet ready to admit is the all-crucial dictum that *ubi Petrus, ibi Ecclesia.*

If we turn now to the book of essays entitled *Christian Reflections*, we find Lewis again dodging the problem. In his introduction, Walter Hooper narrates the following:

I should now, before introducing the papers in this book, like to record to Lewis's credit a positive restraint which he put upon all his theological works. As he was minded to write only about 'mere' Christianity, so he steadfastly refused to write about *differences* of belief. He knew that discussions (or, more likely, arguments) about differences in doctrine or ritual were seldom edifying. At least he considered it far too dangerous a luxury for himself—far better stick to that "enormous common ground."

He made no exception even in his conversation, a fact I know to my own shame. I remember the first (and only) time I mentioned 'low' and 'high' churchmanship in his presence. He looked at me as though I had offered him poison. "We must *never* discuss that," he said, gently but firmly. Again, shortly before the publication of *Honest to God* in the United States, the editor of a popular American magazine asked Lewis to write a critique of the book for his columns. Lewis wrote back: "What would you yourself think of me if I did?. . . . A great deal of my utility has depended on my having kept out of dog-fights between professing schools of 'Christian' thought. I'd sooner preserve that abstinence to the end." This "abstinence" has surely not weakened our conception of the Faith; his salutary single-mindedness has, rather, shown us its balance and true colours such as (I believe) few Christian apologists have succeeded in doing. Lewis, I think, understood very well what diet Our Lord intended when He commanded the Apostle "*Feed* my sheep."[10]

Now compare that with the last paragraph of "Modern Theology and Biblical Criticism." Lewis has been warning his listeners against liberalism in modern theology. He concludes the essay with,

Such are the reactions of one bleating layman to Modern Theology. It is right you should hear them. You will not perhaps hear them very often again. Your parishioners will not often speak to you quite frankly. Once the layman was anxious to hide the fact that he believed so much less than the Vicar: he now tends to hide the fact that he believes so much more. Missionary to the priests of one's own church is an embarrassing rôle; though I have a horrid feeling that if such mission work is not soon undertaken the future history of the Church of England is likely to be short.[11]

Here the essential ingredients of the problem are stated quite succinctly. Lewis is willing to lock horns with the liberals who are not prepared to accept the "mere" Christianity he offers, but if the traditionalists feel that his "mere" Christianity omits or underplays some important things (church, sacraments, Mass, the role of Mary), then we "must never discuss that." He is in precisely the same position that the younger Newman was in before he became aware that "Rome will be found right after all" and that actually there *is* no middle ground. The rug Lewis pretends to be standing on has been pulled from under him; more precisely, there was no rug to begin with.

Writing to Sister Penelope CSMV (8 November 1939), Lewis asserted that he was not a "High" Anglican. "To me the real distinction is not between high and low," he declares, "but between religion with a real supernaturalism and salvationism on the one hand, and all watered-down and modernist versions on the other."[12]

A somewhat fuller treatment of the Church appears in a letter "To a Lady" dated 7 December 1950. "We must be regular practising members of the Church. . . . For the Church is not a human society of people united by their natural affinities but the Body of Christ, in which all members . . . share the common life. . . . If people like you and me find much that we don't naturally like in the public and corporate side of Christianity all the better for us; it will teach us humility and charity. . . ." Here, Lewis is at pains to refute the idea that the Church is a covenant of believers or a society of the elect. Whether Roman or Anglican, his position on the nature of the church is "catholic." But in an undated letter to the same lady, who must have annoyed him by asking why he had not become a Roman Catholic, Lewis somewhat petulantly replied: "The question for me (naturally) is not 'Why should I not be a Roman Catholic' but 'Why should I?' But I don't like discussing such matters, because it emphasizes differences and endangers charity. By the time I had really explained my objections to certain doctrines which differentiate you from us (and also in my opinion from the Apostolic and even the Medieval Church), you would like me less."[13]

This is an interesting letter for several reasons. First, Lewis is clearly on the defensive. Second, he falls back on his customary position of endangering charity. Third, he begs the question somewhat condescendingly, and implies there is a difference between the apostolic church and the Roman church. As for the medieval church, he is clearly thinking of the later historical doctrines with regard to the Virgin Mary and the infallibility of the Pope. Lewis has no clear idea of the magisterium of the Church nor of the development of doctrine, especially intrinsic as opposed to extrinsic development. But he does seem to betray an uneasiness with these questions, even while attempting to dismiss them as not part of "mere" Christianity. Yet they *are* part of mere Christianity, since belief in the Gospel requires the authoritative endorsement of the Church.

In another undated letter to the same lady, Lewis raises the question of Ave Marias, or of the propriety of saluting the Virgin Mary. His objection here is that worship is too easily diverted from the Creator to a creature and opens the door to idolatry. He offers this as an additional reason for his not becoming a Roman Catholic. And yet he is bothered by the divisions in the Church of England; the actuality of the divided Church jars his idealized picture of the Church militant.

The nineteenth letter in *Letters to Malcolm: Chiefly on Prayer* comes to grips with an interpretation of Holy Communion. Here Lewis is at his worst. First, he declares that he is not good enough at theology. He *is*, and has written enough books to prove it. Second, he "could wish that no definitions had ever been felt to be necessary; and, still more, that none had been allowed to make divisions between churches."[14] But this would obviate the necessity for any definitions of the Trinity, the two natures of Christ, and the whole process of the development of the history of Christian thought. The sad thing is that Lewis is no historian. He recognizes a general process called history, but he does not think its specifics are important. Finally, he makes an absurdity of Aristotle's theory of substance and accidents. He cannot imagine a substance stripped of its accidents and endowed with something else. But no one can imagine this. It is a matter of the intellect and not of the imagination. It is *fides quaerens intellectum*, but the Real Presence always remains a mystery. Lewis knows that; all the less reason for his silly anti-intellectual polemic in this nineteenth letter.

Mere Christianity is the fullest statement (and the most concise) of Lewis's religious position. The Church, we learn in "Christian Behaviour," is the whole body of practising Christians. It is not the primary problem of the Church to lay out blueprints for social reform. The Church is primarily geared for the sanctification of its individual members.[15] Again, in "Beyond Personality," Lewis states: "The Church exists for nothing else but to draw men into Christ, to make them little Christs. If they are not doing that, all the cathedrals, clergy, missions, sermons, even the Bible itself, are simply a waste of time. God became Man for no other purpose."[16]

In *Reflections on the Psalms* (chapter 12, "Second Meanings in the Psalms"), Lewis introduces the idea of the Church as a bride, spouse of the bridegroom who is the heavenly King. The Church is called out from the world, she is to leave all that she has known in order to follow the King. "Turn your back" on all that you have known is indeed a terrible command, but the consolation is, "I will make of thee a great nation." Psalm 45 thus contains the second meaning of the Church as bride: one obedient to and worshipful of her Lord the Bridegroom.[17]

In the "Literary Impact of the Authorised Version" (*They Asked for a Paper*), Lewis points out that the Church was not guided by literary principles in its selection of Sacred Scripture. Here he implicitly concedes the fact that Scripture is the product of the Church, and, like Augustine, we believe the Scriptures only because the Church teaches them to be true. He seems to accept the priority of the Church; the Scriptures do not authenticate themselves.

In "Transposition," an essay in *The Weight of Glory*, Lewis talks about glossalalia in the Church, beginning with the experience at Pentecost. This essay shows how important Lewis thought the Church was in the life of every Christian. In "Membership" (*The Weight of Glory*), the idea of the Church as the bride of Christ recurs, and here in this essay we have a fairly articulated idea of the Church as the body of Christ.

> It is in fact that Body of which the family is an image on the natural level. If anyone came to it with the misconception that membership of the Church was membership in a debased modern sense—a massing together of persons as if they were pennies or counters—he would be corrected at the threshold by the discovery that the Head of this Body is so unlike the inferior members that they share no predicate with Him save by analogy. We are summoned from the outset to combine as creatures with our Creator, as mortals with immortal, as redeemed sinners with sinless Redeemer. . . . any conception of Christian fellowship which does not mean primarily fellowship with Him is out of court. After that it seems almost trivial to trace further down the diversity of operations to the unity of the Spirit. But it is very plainly there. There are priests divided from the laity, catechumens divided from those who are in full fellowship. There is authority of husbands over wives and parents over children. There is, in forms too subtle for official embodiment, a continual interchange of complementary ministrations. We are all constantly teaching and learning, forgiving and being forgiven, representing Christ to man when we intercede, and man to Christ when others intercede for us. The sacrifice of selfish privacy which is daily demanded of us is daily repaid a hundredfold in the true growth of personality which the life of the Body encourages. Those who are members of one another become as diverse as the hand and the ear. That is why the worldlings are so monotonously alike compared with the almost fantastic variety of the saints. Obedi-

ence is the road to freedom, humility the road to pleasure, unity the road to personality.[18]

This is one of the most continuous sections on the Church that Lewis wrote, although he oscillates between the visible body of Christ and the invisible. It is an essentially Pauline view as found in First Corinthians 12.

The essay of Dom Bede Griffiths in Jim Como's *C. S. Lewis at the Breakfast Table* ("The Adventure of Faith" is Father Griffiths's title) will serve to bring this chapter to a conclusion. Both Lewis and Griffiths were becoming Christians at the same time. When Griffiths became a Catholic, however, Lewis failed to follow the "argument to its logical conclusion." Griffiths says that Lewis had an almost total lack of concern about the Church as an institution. "To me," Lewis wrote in *Surprised by Joy*, "religion ought to have been a matter of good men praying alone, and meeting by twos and threes to talk of spiritual matters." And again, "The idea of churchmanship was to me wholly unattractive." It was the externals of church worship that he found so unattractive, "a kind of wearisome, get-together affair." Hymns and organ music were also especially unappealing. "Hymns were (and are) extremely disagreeable to me. Of all musical instruments I liked (and like) the organ least."[19]

Griffiths goes on to say that it "is remarkable also that Lewis showed very little interest in the Fathers of the Church. . . . Apart from mention of Saint Augustine's *Confessions*, I don't remember his ever referring to one of the Fathers."[20] This would suggest that Lewis had very little sense of the Church as a living organism, growing by stages through the centuries, as Newman portrayed it in his "Development of Christian Doctrine." Griffiths adds that Lewis was most unsympathetic to the revival of Thomism, and felt that any renewal or revival of scholasticism was surely only a fad which would soon be discarded.

While making a casual remark about Richard Hooker (whom Lewis treats admirably in *English Literature in the Sixteenth Century*), Griffiths sums up the situation perfectly: "The concept of the Church as the Mystical Body of Christ (which I had discovered first in Hooker, for whom we both shared a great admiration) had been the leading motive in my becoming a Catholic. . . . Lewis was later to acquire a deep reverence for and understanding of the mystery of the Eucharist, but this aspect of the Church as a worshipping community and of cult as something 'sacred,' a reflection on earth of a heavenly reality, remained hidden from him."[21]

And why? My concluding judgment is that it was due to Lewis's having no sense of, and no interest in, history. His literary criticisms were divorced from concurrent political history. And the larger social, economic, cultural and church history he missed altogether. His blind spot on music may be forgiven, but his historical blind spot, never! In a word, he had not sufficiently pondered his John Henry Newman.

Scripture and Prayer

Lewis never worked out a systematic approach to the nature of Scripture. His position on this subject must be deduced from the rest of his theological teaching, as Michael J. Christensen has aptly pointed out in his *C. S. Lewis on Scripture*.[1] Both liberals and conservatives claim that Lewis belongs to them, but it is the opinion of this writer that Lewis almost always articulates the traditional position of the Anglo-Catholic church, which stands nearer to the Roman Catholic church than to any other. On 18 November 1965 the Second Vatican Council issued its Dogmatic Constitution on Divine Revelation, which has considerable to say about Scripture. Lewis had died just two years before, but his ideas so nearly approach the position of Vatican II that he might well have subscribed to it with very little qualification.

Lewis believed that the Bible was inspired. "If every good and perfect gift comes from the Father of Lights then all true and edifying writings, whether in Scripture or not, must be *in some sense*-inspired."[2] This is not to say that all parts of the Bible are equally inspired (Lewis thinks not) but that the divine element is the result of the work of the Holy Spirit. The traditional position has always been that the Scriptures have God as their author, nor is it likely that Lewis would deny this.

The crucial question for Lewis is, How is the Bible inspired? and this leads him to embark on an analysis of literary criticism. After all, Lewis was primarily a literary critic even before he was a theologian, so naturally "to understand the Bible correctly it is necessary to study its literary form. For example, the question about Jonah and the great fish does not turn simply on intrinsic probability. The point is that the whole Book of Jonah has the air of being a moral romance, a quite different kind of thing from, say, the account of King David or the New Testament, not pegged like them into any historical situation. There are different kinds of narrative in the Bible; surely it would be illogical to suppose that these different kinds should all be read in the same way."[3]

Hence he rules out the view that every statement in Scripture must be historical truth. One must ask what the writer intends. The figure of Jonah may or may not be historical, but that question is of secondary importance. The primary aim of the writer was to underscore some religious or moral truth. Lewis is not a fundamentalist. It is not the medium through which the message comes that is inspired; it is the message. And it is primarily the message of salvation and God's revelation of himself in Jesus Christ. These great themes of redemption are far more important than whether or not Elisha's ax head floated (2 Kings 6:6).

While he believed Scripture was undoubtedly inspired, Lewis never intended to limit inspiration to Scripture alone. God reveals Himself in literary masterpieces, other religions, myths, reason and nature (and Lewis might have added art and music). Truth can be found in all these vehicles, but one cannot expect a different kind of truth from that which is ostensibly offered. "The kind of truth we demand of Scripture," Lewis states, "was in my opinion never even envisaged by the ancients."[4]

As a literary critic, Lewis thought the same principles of interpretation should apply to the Bible as to anything else. Therefore he endorsed textual criticism in order to establish the trustworthiness of biblical documents and texts; yet he had a low opinion of source criticism because he thought it often impossible to determine what influenced the writer, what sources he used, and the whole Sitz-im-Leben of the text. A personal incident in which he himself had been totally misunderstood in an essay on William Morris convinced him that much modern higher criticism should be both irrelevant and misleading.[5]

In his essay entitled "Modern Theology and Biblical Criticism," Lewis faults some liberal critics for claiming too little for historicity and too much for poetry. "If he tells me that something in a Gospel is legend or romance, I want to know how many legends and romances he has read, how well his palate is trained in detecting them by the flavour; not how many years he has spent on that Gospel."[6] Lewis thus holds for the historicity of the Fourth Gospel, and indeed the entire New Testament for that matter. When the evangelists admit evidence which is damaging to their cause or embarrassing to their position, we almost certainly have historical accuracy. In fact, Lewis would hold for considerable historicity in the Old Testament as well.

Yet Lewis has a deep appreciation for the role of myth in the Bible. By myth he does not mean falsehood or some tale made up of "whole cloth," but rather a "likely story" in the Platonic sense. The importance of myth is that it is a via media between meaningless abstraction on the one hand and a crass literalism on the other. The early stories in Genesis properly fall under the category of myth. In *The Pilgrim's Regress*, Lewis writes, "Mythology . . . is but truth, not fact: an image, not the very real. But then it is My mythology . . . this is the veil under which I have chosen to appear even from the first until now. For this end I made your senses and for this end your imagination, that you might see My face and live."[7] In his essay entitled "Myth Became Fact" Lewis says, "In the enjoyment of a great myth we come nearest to experiencing as a concrete what can otherwise be understood only as an abstraction."[8]

The most important use of myth is in the creation stories of Genesis and the temptation and fall of man. It is generally agreed that Lewis is reluctant to accept the Adam and Eve story as historical fact, but is convinced that the story is symbolically true. In *The Problem of Pain*, he offers his own version of what may have happened.

> For long centuries God perfected the animal form which was to become the vehicle of humanity and the image of Himself. He gave it hands whose thumb could be applied to each of the fingers, and jaws and teeth and throat capable of articulation, and a brain sufficiently complex to execute all the material motions whereby rational thought is incarnated. The creature may have existed for ages in this state before it became man: it may even have been clever enough to make things which a modern archaeologist would accept as proof of its humanity. But it was only an animal because all its physical and psychical processes were directed to purely material and natural ends. Then, in the fullness of time, God caused to descend upon this organism, both on its psychology and physiology, a new kind of consciousness which could say "I" and "me," which could look upon itself as an object, which knew God, which could make judgments of truth, beauty, and goodness, and which was so far above time that it could perceive time flowing past. This new consciousness ruled and illuminated the whole organism. . . .
>
> I do not doubt that if the Paradisal man could now appear among us, we should regard him as an utter savage, a creature to be exploited or, at best, patronised. Only one or two, and those the holiest among us, would glance a second time at the naked, shaggy-bearded, slow-spoken creature: but they, after a few minutes, would fall at his feet.
>
> We do not know how many of these creatures God made, nor how long they continued in the Paradisal state. But sooner or later they fell. Someone or something whispered that they could become as gods. . . .[9]

This is a fine use of myth or symbolic truth, possibly but not necessarily based on historical fact, conveying a universal idea in the dress of fantasy. It involves the use of "baptized imagination" and functions as a bridge between the infinite realm of Absolute Reality and the finite realm of abstract, propositional truth.[10] "Myth," says Lewis, "is the mountain whence all the different streams arise which become truths down here in the valley; *in hac valle abstractionis* [in this valley of separation]. Or, if you prefer, myth is the isthmus which connects the peninsular world of thought with that vast continent we really belong to."[11]

Why can we not say that the resurrection stories are also myth? Because, Lewis replies, the writers clearly do not intend them as such. The resurrection of Jesus is an actual event in history which at the same time must be taken on faith. The Gospel writers clearly intend that their message be understood as historical fact. But neither must everything be understood in a literal sense. Lewis feels that here the Scripture authenticates itself with an intrinsic authority; he never appeals to an extrinsic authority such as the magisterium of the Church as the proper interpreter of Scripture. He may not have believed this, he may not have thought that such an appeal was necessary, or he may have discarded the idea as not consonant with "mere" Christianity. But by not making such an appeal, it seems to this writer that he weakens his case.

We now need to say a word about inerrancy. Christensen points out that Lewis believed that not only were the biblical writers inspired, but the editors, copyists and translators who modified the original writings were supernaturally guided by God as well. The end product can therefore be accepted as fully inspired, reliable and authoritative.[12] Inerrancy really should apply to the Bible taken as a whole. It announces the Good News of our salvation, and in this respect it teaches nothing false. Insofar as it deals with history, politics or science, its aim is to teach truth, but truth with a religious bias. After all, we are dealing here with the Word of God, although the Word of God is more properly the ongoing revelation in Jesus Christ. Certainly the Bible has its human side, but it never intends to convey information which does not have a religious purpose. The curtain of truth has been torn at one edge to reveal our immediate practical necessities and not to satisfy our intellectual curiosity.

These then are some tentative thoughts (as he himself put it) that Lewis held on Scripture. As has been stated, he concurs more or less with the Vatican II statement, so if one is to use Protestant terminology he cannot be classed as either a fundamentalist or a liberal. His failure to work out a complete system in this area would seem to indicate that he did not think it held the highest priority.

Although Lewis did not take up the subject of Scripture at length, he did devote one whole book to the subject of prayer: *Letters to Malcolm: Chiefly on Prayer*. Chiefly, but not entirely, for random thoughts on quite different subjects also emerge from time to time. Lewis's bête noire, liberal Christianity, even bobs up at the end of the book for its customary castigation. It was to be Lewis's last book, and appeared posthumously. The letters are casual but intimate, flowing easily, but also carrying at times quite heavy cargo. Malcolm is a purely fictitious character, as are his wife Betty and their son George. Perhaps the phenomenal success of *The Screwtape Letters* suggested to Lewis a return to this literary form; if so, the original stylistic success was not repeated. The rather heavy content of the letters combined with what often seems like a frivolous manner sometimes produces a feeling of discomfort. Be that as it may, the task here is to outline briefly some of Lewis's thoughts and attitudes toward prayer.

We are to understand that it is private, not corporate prayer which is under discussion. Lewis was not interested in liturgy per se; he thought it ought to be as unobtrusive as possible, to serve as a means to worship, not be an end in itself. He disliked liturgical novelties, and music did not play an important part in his life. While public worship was certainly important, Lewis felt that private prayer was more important. And this is what the *Letters* concentrate on.

Prayer must be undergirded with sound doctrine so that we know what we may ask for. Keeping this in mind, it does not matter so much whether we use set forms of prayer (such as the Lord's Prayer), compose our own, or even pray without using words at all. But when addressing the Infinite, what is the proper stance? Is it one of familiarity or non-familiarity? Is there an intimacy between the participants or a great distance impossible to cross. Lewis tries to hold on to both these elements in prayer; there is a certain amount of ceremonial which is necessary, yet we are also sons of a loving heavenly Father. In fact, he says that prayer may be like making love to one's wife!

A more important point for Lewis is the importance of posture in prayer. Proper posture creates proper reverence and proper concentration. Nor should prayer be left until one's bedtime. It requires a clear mind and a relaxed body in order to be effective, and one must have the ability to remove distractions. Later on, Lewis will discuss the Ignatian principle of putting one's self into a "composition of place," although he feels that modern scholarship has made this difficult for twentieth-century man. He also averts to the necessity of putting one's self in the presence of God, although this, too, requires patience and practice, and for modern man may not be altogether successful. What seems to escape Lewis entirely, at least according to the Ignatian method of prayer, is the necessity for determining some particular fruit or some special grace that one seeks from God.

Perhaps this is not altogether fair to Lewis. One of the Ignatian principles of prayer is to seek a specific spiritual or temporal gift or grace—sometimes called the *id quod volo* (what I specifically

desire from the meditation)—and certainly Lewis believes in re-
questing temporal as well as spiritual things; but he does not quite
put the two together so that the purpose of the meditation or prayers is to obtain that which one seeks or desires. But we must not
expect a thoroughly worked-out doctrine of spirituality in twenty-
two brief, almost casual, letters.

Petitionary prayer involves making our requests known to God.
But what is the sense of telling God what he already knows? The
answer here seems to be that prayer makes a change in the pray-er,
that God is thus able to "reveal" himself to the petitioner who has
been changed by his prayer. But prayers must be legitimate; we
must free ourselves from inordinate attachments and silly requests.
Our desires must be legitimate desires and we must pray for them,
putting ourselves "on a personal footing with God."[18]

The fifth letter to Malcolm deals in large part with the Lord's
Prayer and Lewis's interpretation of this classic model of petitionary prayer. He points out that "Thy will be done" is to be
understood in an active as well as a passive sense. We are not
merely to make acts of resignation in times of difficulty or suffering, but we are to be actively engaged in the carrying out of the
divine plan. This is what Lewis calls a "festoon," a sort of spiritual embellishment of a personal nature. This opens the door to
one of his favorite themes, the "sin" of expecting a pleasure to
repeat itself. What he is saying here is that we must submit ourselves, surrender ourselves to future joys and blessings; we must
not expect them to be mere reduplications of past experiences. In
Perelandra one never experiences the repetition of a wave. We fail
to receive many blessings from God because we are often on the
lookout for some other blessing, a duplication of something we
have experienced in the past. And so in our lack of self-surrender,
we fail to do the will of God in an active sense.

The most difficult part of the Lord's Prayer is the injunction to forgive. Lewis says, "To forgive for the moment is not difficult. But to go on forgiving, to forgive the same offence again every time it recurs to the memory—there's the real tussle."[14] The cure is to offset one's personal grievances with the recollection of the numbers of times we have "bullied" others. This at least makes for humility.

The section on petitionary prayer concludes with a discussion of the predictable universe vis-à-vis human freedom. Granted that the resolution of these two seemingly opposed factors is a divine mystery, it is important to put the mystery at the right spot. Without entering the sticky argument of divine concursus, it is somehow possible to reconcile man's freedom with the orderly structure of the universe. What Lewis argues here is that the predictability of the universe may be overrated, and that as a result petitionary prayer can be a real force in a world in which freedom may lie at its very center. And here let the matter rest.

Unanswered prayer presents a challenge to faith. It may be true that when God does not answer our prayers in the way we would wish, he gives us something better. It may be true that to answer our prayer in the way we would wish would be a personal disaster. It may also be true that too often our sins stand in the way of God. Lewis makes much of the fact that Our Lord's prayer in Gethsemane was not answered. Of course the words "if it be thy will" were added to the request that the cup pass from him, but it may be that our prayers are more often not granted than fulfilled. This is more apt to be true, Lewis thinks, as we advance in spirituality; the consolations of beginners were never meant to last. But again it is important to remember that prayer changes the pray-er. Ultimately there is no answer to unanswered prayer, and every soul must at one time drain the cup of dereliction and cry out in anguish, "My God, my God, why hast thou forsaken me?"

Lewis's fullest exposition of the subject of miracles is in a book

by that name, but the subject comes up with regard to prayer. Do
not miracles step outside the usual cause and effect relationship?
And cannot the same thing be said about prayer? How can we be
sure that what happens to us as a result of prayer would not have
happened to us anyhow? But if all this were true, then prayer
would be meaningless, and we are certainly taught to pray, to pray
without ceasing. It must be, then, that everything is providential
and every act of God a special providence. "One of the purposes
for which God instituted prayer may have been to bear witness
that the course of events is not governed like a state but created
like a work of art to which every being makes its contribution and
(in prayer) a conscious contribution, and in which every being is
both an end and a means."[15]

The Gospels tell us that whatever we ask for in prayer, believing
that we receive it, will be granted to us. How does this square with
the observed facts, and most of all with the unanswered prayer
in Gethsemane? Lewis can only guess at the answer. A suitor in
prayer is one who makes a specific request of the Lord, a servant
is one who carries out his orders, a friend is one who is let in on
the Master's secrets. One is a friend of God if he is a prophet, an
apostle, a missionary, a healer; these are the people who can in
mountaintop experiences ask anything to the removing of mountains. So, perhaps it is the very advanced in the spiritual life to
whom these particular verses are addressed. And along with this
goes always the struggle for faith, to believe that God does hear us
and can answer our requests, and that we are not wasting our time
by addressing an empty universe.

Prayer may lead one to the mystical experience, which may by
no means be an illusion. Now there may be diabolical mysticism,
or a mysticism produced by drugs, but what is important for Lewis
is not the experience so much as where it leads. "The lawfulness,
safety, and utility of the mystical voyage depends not at all on its

being mystical—that is, on its being a departure—but on the motives, skill, and constancy of the voyager, and on the grace of God." Again, "Departures are all alike; it is the landfall that crowns the voyage. The saint, by being a saint, proves that his mysticism (if he was a mystic; not all saints are) led him aright; the fact that he has practiced mysticism could never prove his sanctity."[16] One does not set out to have a mystical experience, which after all is really a gift of God. One sets out in humble and selfless love; the result is no longer in human hands.

Prayers for others tend to flow more freely than prayers for ourselves. This may look like charity, but it may be just easier to pray for people than to do things for them. "It's so much easier to pray for a bore than to go and see him." It also requires no moral effort on my part to pray for you to avoid your besetting sin. In other words, praying for one's self may require a reformation of character! Praying for others may seem to require the keeping of interminable prayer lists, but by concentrating on God one automatically keeps in mind the person to be prayed for. It doesn't, however, work the other way around.

Is the ideal prayer really a soliloquy? One thinks of Saint Augustine's *Confessions*, which is actually a long prayer addressed to God. Lewis's answer would be affirmative; prayer is somehow God speaking to God. "He is always both within us and over against us. Our reality is so much from His reality as He, moment by moment, projects into us. The deeper the level within ourselves from which our prayer, or any other act, wells up, the more it is His, but not at all the less ours. Rather, most ours when most His."[17] Creator and creature interact in some mysterious way.

But why does God decide to act through creatures when he could do a better job by acting alone? Why should God speak to himself through man? Lewis answers that all of creation is a delegation of powers, and that God does nothing that he cannot do through creatures. In "Beyond Personality," Lewis discussed the difference between making and begetting. Here the point being made is that God is a giver; he delegates his power to creatures and in this way he gives himself. One must remember that creation has been brought into existence *out of nothing*. This is not to say that there was some previous matter out of which God formed the universe. Before the universe was created, *nothing* existed. In pantheism, God is all. But the whole point of creation surely is that he was not content to be all. He intends to be "all *in all*."[18]

Creation is therefore other than God. We can never confuse the creation with the Creator. He is in creation, but he is *not* in creation. Of each creature, we can say: "This also is Thou; neither is this Thou." On the one hand we must emphasize the transcendence of God, on the other the fact that God is in all things. He is more in a tree than in a rock, more in a man than in a beast; but also as we go up the scale, the more the creature can wield its little trident. Trees and animals cannot sin; men and women can sin grievously.

Practicing the presence of God is a familiar stepping stone in the spiritual life, but Lewis points out that we often practice the evasion of God. We are reminded of Francis Thompson's *Hound of Heaven*. The presence of God which we often voluntarily evade is God's presence in wrath. He comes to rebuke as well as console. He is not a safe God, he is not a tame God, anymore than the Pevensie children found Aslan a safe or a tame lion. But if God comes neither to console nor to rebuke, it may be that we have begun to lose him altogether.

Lewis devotes considerable discussion to the use of mental images in prayer. The Ignatian principle of a composition of place he does not find altogether helpful for various reasons. (It should be noted that Saint Ignatius did not always recommend using a composition of place.) Lewis fears that the composition of place may either be unreal or so real that the meditation proper is never reached at all. Mental images do play an important part in prayer, but he feels they are most helpful when they are fugitive and fragmentary. They are to be valued mostly for their qualitative value, and kissed (as Blake says) when they fly by. It is not altogether clear what Lewis means, and once again I would urge that what he misses is the importance of seeking a specific fruit, a grace, an insight, an act of the will, the Ignatian *id quod volo* which is indeed a real part of the meditation, if not its purpose.

Prayer also involves worship and adoration. Beginning where we are, we give thanks for the beauties of nature and the joy of everyday things which point us to the means of grace and the hope of glory. Joy is the serious business of heaven. Pleasures are the shafts of the glory as it strikes our sensibility. Every pleasure can be a channel of adoration. "At thy right hand there are pleasures forevermore," is a text that Lewis never tires of quoting. (Ps. 16: 11). Pleasures have the breath of divinity about them, but one must not be greedy for them; it is fatal to shout "encore" rather than to "kiss them in flight." Pure and spontaneous pleasures are "patches of Godlight" in the woods of our experience. Even such seemingly frivolous things as dances and games may exist in heaven where they are not frivolous, for that is their natural home.

Prayer involves repentance. However, Lewis objects to those authors who tell us that we ought always to be contemplating our total depravity. Certainly a spiritual emetic at the right moment is worthwhile, but a steady diet of emetics? Lewis thinks not; he is no Puritan subscribing to a constant examination of one's own corruption. When we glimpse this corruption, then indeed there must be prayers of repentance leading to acts of repentance. Only in this way can we prepare ourselves for the reception of pardon. But to look for and dwell on the "slimy things" deep inside us is to look away from "the New Testament fruits of the spirit—love, joy, peace. And very unlike the Pauline programme; 'forgetting those things which are behind and reaching forth unto those things that are before.' . . . This poring over the 'sink' might breed its own perverse pride."[19]

We cannot understand the real meaning of sin because it is a mystery. We must contemplate the Cross if we want to know what God thinks of iniquity. The Bible speaks of God's wrath, but this is only analogical. To Lewis it is analogous to the strongest human emotion. "Anger—no peevish fit of temper, but just, generous, scalding indignation—passes (not necessarily at once) into embracing, exultant, re-welcoming love. That is how friends and lovers are truly reconciled. Hot wrath, hot love. Such anger is the fluid love bleeds when you cut it. The *angers*, not the measured remonstrances, of lovers are love's renewal. Wrath and pardon are both, as applied to God, analogies; but they belong to the same circle of analogy—the circle of life, and love, and deeply personal relationships."[20]

Lest his remarks on prayer seem too private and insufficient in their emphasis upon community, Lewis ties the life of prayer to the reception of Holy Communion—an intensely personal act for him. Mention has already been made of his detachment if not indifference to public liturgy, and his remarks about the Eucharist are devotional, not theological. The command, after all (he reminds us) was take, eat; not take, understand.[21] Begging off from a discussion of the Eucharist on the grounds that he is not a good enough theologian (false modesty), he concludes his observations on repentance with an underscoring of the necessity of personal forgiveness in our human relations. After all, the Lord's Prayer makes a key point of this.

Lewis approves of praying for the dead. But the traditional Protestant view is that the dead are already either saved or damned, and hence prayers for them would be useless. This forces Lewis to acknowledge a belief in purgatory, or at least in some time-place where the soul may be completely cleansed. This will probably involve suffering, although suffering is not the purpose of purgation. The treatment given will be the one required, whether it hurts little or much. Nor do we know whether or not this process goes on in time, or whether the dead themselves are in time. An omnipotent Creator is quite able to dovetail the spiritual and physical histories of the world into each other. The upshot of all this is that prayers for the deceased are only natural, and, indeed, the older we get the longer the list of our dear departed.

Acknowledging the irksomeness of prayer, the duty of it and the drudgery involved, the tendency to crowd it off the page entirely, and the wearisome dryness which often accompanies it, we are warned not to skimp and begrudge this aspect of the spiritual life. Much of our avoidance may be due to our sins, but there is also the reluctance not to come face to face with the Eternal. Yet the painful effort which prayer involves does not mean that we are doing something we were not created to do. The truth is, prayer ought to be a delight, and perhaps some day it will be. At present, Lewis says, we are still schoolboys—but we shall not be forever. What is drudgery and dryness today will not be so tomorrow. And our worst prayers—those which are supported by the least devotional feeling and accompanied with the greatest disinclination—may be in God's eyes our best. After all, feelings can be largely a gift; it is the inclination of the will which really counts.

The *Letters to Malcolm* do not pretend to be an exhaustive or even a systematic treatment of prayer. Indeed, as earlier mentioned, other topics are occasionally introduced—very often doctrinal ones. Lewis does not believe that doctrine and prayer can be separated; right prayer demands right belief and right belief means avoiding the demythologizing tendencies of liberal Christianity. But these topics are insufficient to bring the series to a final focus, or a convincing conclusion. Lewis chooses to do this by emphasizing the supernatural dimensions of our lives: the reality of Heaven and the resurrection of the body (and that means the resurrection of the senses). At some future date we shall return and reassume the wealth we have laid down. "Then the new earth and sky, the same yet not the same as these, will rise in us as we have risen in Christ. And once again, after who knows what aeons of the silence and the dark, the birds will sing and the waters flow, and lights and shadows move across the hills, and the faces of our friends laugh upon us with amazed recognition."[22]

Ethics

The best discussion of Lewis's social and ethical thought is to be found in Gilbert Meilaender's *The Taste for the Other*. Meilaender starts his excellent book by taking issue with Chad Walsh's statement in his *C. S. Lewis: Apostle to the Skeptics* that "for a Christian social philosophy one turns to Maritain, Niebuhr, Berdyaev, George McLeod, and many others—not to C. S. Lewis."[1] Meilaender's rejoinder to this statement is this: "If he means that Lewis seldom gives specific answers to concrete problems, we may grant the point—although we may also wonder whether all of those Walsh names offer, for the most part, anything more than a theological framework within which one may think about politics and society."[2] Although Lewis's ethic is largely personal (as Meilaender's book inadvertently shows), nonetheless it is by no means devoid of social implications, which in some instances (marriage, family, sex) are spelled out quite clearly.

I shall attempt no more than a summary and evaluation of Lewis's social and ethical position, since all admit that his forte does not lie here; in the areas of economics and politics he had neither expertise nor interest, and he was almost contemptuous of sociology. We have discussed the fact that he had little interest in political history. He does have a philosophy of history (as we shall see), but it is correct to say that in several areas his social ethic is implied rather than specifically articulated. Whether those whom Walsh has enumerated have done a better job at it (Niebuhr probably has) is, of course, beside the point.

A good place to begin is with the concept of the *tao* or what the Western world calls (roughly) the natural law. The first quarter of *Mere Christianity* ("Right and Wrong as a Clue to the Meaning of the Universe") is the *locus classicus* for this idea, along with *The Abolition of Man*, a short book which explicitates the notion of natural law in some detail.

In all of this, Lewis shows himself a child of Plato; the present age is corroded with subjectivity, and mankind must return to objective standards regarding moral judgments if it is to survive. These objective standards are written into the very fabric of the universe and they are the way (tao) which must be followed if man is not to destroy himself. The very first lines of *Mere Christianity* set the stage for Lewis's fundamental point of view:

> Everyone has heard people quarrelling. Sometimes it sounds funny and sometimes it sounds merely unpleasant; but however it sounds, I believe we can learn something very important from listening to the kinds of things they say. They say things like this: "How'd you like it if anyone did the same as you?"—"That's my seat, I was there first" —"Leave him alone, he isn't doing you any harm"—"Why should you shove in first?"—"Give me a bit of your orange, I gave you a bit of mine"—"Come on, you promised." People say things like that every day, educated people as well as uneducated, and children as well as grownups.

> Now what interests me about all these remarks is that the man who makes them is not merely saying that the other man's behaviour does not happen to please him. He is appealing to some kind of standard of behaviour which he expects the other man to know about. And the other man very seldom replies: "To hell with your standard." Nearly always he tries to make out that what he has been doing does not really go against the standard, or that if it does there is some special excuse. . . .[3]

This standard of behavior has been acknowledged by people in all times and places. The early Hindus called it the *rita*—"that great ritual or pattern of nature and supernature which is revealed alike in the cosmic order, the moral virtues, and the ceremonial of the temple." The Chinese called it the tao—"the reality beyond all predicates, the abyss that was before the Creator Himself. It is Nature . . . it is the way in which the universe goes on, the Way in which things everlastingly emerge, stilly and tranquilly, into space and time. The ancient Jews likewise praise the Law as being 'true.' " In short, "it is the doctrine of objective value, the belief that certain attitudes are really true, and others really false, to the kind of thing the universe is and the kind of things we are."[4]

A favorite example Lewis uses is that of the Roman father telling his son that it is a sweet and fitting thing to die for one's country. The point is that this injunction cannot be defended on the grounds of mere sentiment. A noble death illustrates an objective value which cannot be defended on the grounds of subjective sentimentality. In battle, what keeps us at our posts in the third hour of bombardment is some conviction born outside of us which goes by the name of duty. "I had sooner play cards against a man who was quite skeptical about ethics, but bred to believe that 'a gentleman does not cheat,' than against an irreproachable moral philosopher who had been brought up among sharpers."[5]

To the objection that different ages and different civilizations have had different moralities, Lewis replies that this is not so. We cannot imagine a society in which cowardice is rewarded or where people feel proud of having double-crossed their benefactors. Nor is the moral law to be confused with herd instinct; herd instinct we may have, but sometimes we do things diametrically opposed to the herd instinct. The moral law carries with it an obligation to act in a certain manner; there is an "ought" which insists on obedience. Granted we do not always follow this law of nature, but still the majority of mankind recognizes its existence.

How does it manifest itself? Lewis writes: "The only way in which we could expect it to show itself would be inside ourselves as an influence or a command trying to get us to behave in a certain way. And that is just what we do find inside ourselves. Surely this ought to arouse our suspicions? In the only case where you can expect to get an answer, the answer turns out to be Yes."[6]

The law of nature, or the moral law, turns out to be the main undergirding of Lewis's ethical position. There is nothing particularly Christian about this; in fact Meilaender calls this the "primeval moral platitudes."[7] But it occurs in virtually all of Lewis's writings. There is a discussion of it in *That Hideous Strength* when Frost tries to rid Mark of all of his "human baggage," including any adherence to the moral law (which Frost calls a system of instinctive preferences), so that he will become totally objective.[8] And in *Out of the Silent Planet*, Oyarsa says to the wicked scientist Weston, "I see now how the lord of the silent world has bent you. There are laws that all *hnau* know, of pity and straight dealing and shame and the like, and one of these is the love of kindred. He has taught you to break all of them except this one, which is not one of the greatest laws; this one he has bent till it becomes folly and has set it up, thus bent, to be a little, blind Oyarsa in your brain. And now you can do nothing but obey it, though if we ask you why it is a law you give no other reason for it than for all the other and greater laws which it drives you to disobey."[9]

For Lewis, these first principles of primeval moral platitudes are self-evident. They are statements of value, not statements of fact. They are given as the moral structure of the universe. Not even God can disobey them. What their relation to God is can be difficult to determine. Are they the arbitrary product of God's will, as Scotus and certainly William of Ockham would maintain? More than likely Lewis holds the Thomistic position that the natural law stems from the Eternal Law, which is God himself. The argument is of no consequence. All that Lewis is saying is what Kant said, that one of the great wonders of the universe is the moral law within.

It is not altogether clear from reason alone what the sanction is when the moral law is broken. To step outside of the tao is to cease to be a member of the human community. It is in a sense to destroy one's self. Christianity is clearer: "the wage paid by sin is death" (Rom. 6:23), and to violate the natural law is to break fellowship with God. For this is the purpose of man's creation—eternal happiness with his Creator.

Lewis summarizes all this in a short paragraph in *Mere Christianity*: "Morality, then, seems to be concerned with three things. Firstly, with fair play and harmony between individuals. Secondly, with what might be called tidying up or harmonizing the things inside each individual. Thirdly, with the general purpose of human life as a whole: what man was made for: what course the whole fleet ought to be on: what tune the conductor of the band wants it to play."[10]

The Chronicles of Narnia very frequently address themselves to the idea of the common good. In *The Voyage of the "Dawn Treader,"* Eustace has to learn to abandon more and more of his selfishness once he realizes how impossible he has been as a member of the sailing expedition. Indeed, community is rooted in the very nature of God himself, for there we have a community of three Divine Persons. The Law of Love requires community in which to operate. In heaven, the notion of the cosmic dance illustrates the importance of community, of mutual self-giving and self-sharing. Just as the different organs of the body cooperate with one another, so must the individual members of society.

Lewis sets his face stoutly against the evils of individualism on the one hand and totalitarianism on the other. Love creates community; without love community is impossible. But individuals need to give love as well as receive it. In *The Discarded Image*, Lewis speaks of the thirsty and aspiring love of creatures for God, as well as God's provident and descending love for creatures.[11] This idea is re-echoed in *The Four Loves*, and indeed is a recurrent theme in many of Lewis's writings.[12] The need for community, however, is all the more urgent today since men and women are estranged from it; the world is marred by sin. Screwtape writes that God "is not content, even Himself, to be a sheer arithmetical unity; He claims to be three as well as one, in order that this nonsense about Love may find a foothold in His own nature. At the other end of the scale, He introduces into matter that obscene invention the organism, in which the parts are perverted from their natural destiny of competition and made to co-operate."[13]

Meilaender points out that Lewis tries to balance two concepts of love: the idea of self-giving or self-sacrifice, and the wishing of good to the neighbor. The first idea is embodied in the celebrated saying that he who loses his life shall find or save it. It is what the spiritual writers have sometimes called *agere contra*, or going against the grain. Its quintessential expression is martyrdom, for which every Christian must at least theoretically be prepared.

Balancing this idea of self-giving is that of wishing the neighbor's good. This is not to say that we must like our neighbor, indeed we may not. But we must love him, and that means to wish him well in positive action for his own good. One's neighbor may be executed, or sent to the front lines, but this does not contradict the principle of wishing his welfare. It is still an expression of love (difficult as this may be to understand) which regards the welfare of the community as well as that of the individual.[14] With these basic suppositions and general guidelines, we can now proceed to examine Lewis's social and ethical thought somewhat more in detail. And that can be done most easily simply by following his section in *Mere Christianity* entitled "Christian Behaviour."

All civilized peoples recognize the "cardinal" or pivotal virtues of prudence, temperance, justice and fortitude; they come to their fullest articulation in the writings of Plato. Prudence means practical common sense, thinking things out ahead of time and weighing the consequences of our actions; temperance means doing nothing in excess, or *tantum quantum* as the Romans would have put it; justice means giving each one his proper due, fairly and honestly; and fortitude refers to courage or bravery under all kinds of stress. Lewis thinks that you cannot practice any of the other virtues very long without bringing this last one into play; he might have gone further and said that all four of the virtues are interdependent on one another. Each of these actions must be performed repeatedly in order to produce their corresponding virtues. Now although the Greeks thought that the virtues were valid for this life only, Christianity holds that we are all going to live forever. It is important to build up these virtues now, since somehow we will possess them in the next life.

In his discussion of social morality, Lewis holds that Christianity is not primarily a new morality; Christ's mission on earth was not merely that of a moral teacher. The world has had moral teachers aplenty, Lewis reminds us, and it has rarely listened to any of them. It was not likely to listen to one more. For this reason we should not look for any startling social or political programs coming from the Church. It is not the prerogative of the clergy to initiate new social systems; that is up to Christian politicians and economists. Time makes ancient good uncouth, Lewis would say, and what is suitable for one society or culture at one specific time may not be for another. "The job is really on us, on the laymen. The application of Christian principles, say, to trade unionism or education must come from trade unionists and Christian schoolmasters: just as Christian literature comes from Christian novelists and dramatists—not from the bench of bishops getting together and trying to write plays and novels in their spare time."[15]

Now, in the areas in which Lewis admittedly had no interest—
political history, economics, and sociology—he tends to give sim-
plistic answers. For instance, Christians can Christianize the political order if there are enough of them, and if they really set their
minds to it. Is this to say that no political system is better than any
other? Lewis emphatically does believe in hierarchy in society, and
The Chronicles of Narnia as well as some other scattered references would seem to indicate a penchant for monarchy. It is true
that the New Testament does not offer us any specific political
program, but Christianity also acknowledges the Old Testament,
which abounds in political observations. The seventeenth century,
for example, was rife with Christians intent on establishing Christian (or more Christian) communities. The Puritans in Massachu-
setts are a fine example of it. The Quakers, the Baptists, the Lev-
ellers, the Diggers, the Fifth Monarchy men all enriched England
with their Christian-political idealism. Lewis betrays preferences
for those political systems which he feels are more intrinsically
Christian. He clearly does not like totalitarianism, for instance.

William Luther White observes in his *The Image of Man in
C. S. Lewis* that

> Lewis's remarks on government were brief and scattered. There are
> two possible reasons, he said, for believing in a democratic form of
> government. One may think that all men are so good that they deserve
> to share in their government and so wise that the government needs
> their advice. Or one may think that fallen men are so wicked that not
> one can be trusted with unlimited power over the others. The first idea
> is a false, romantic notion. The latter idea more nearly resembles the
> truth of man's actual situation. Theocracy, Lewis felt, is the worst pos-
> sible type of government. The loftier the pretensions of any political
> system, the more meddlesome it will be. Political power is always a
> necessary evil, but it is least evil when its sanctions are modest. A
> government should operate with the limited objectives of usefulness
> and convenience for its citizens.[16]

Lewis likewise begs off with a wave of the hand from any attempt
at discussing in depth such thorny matters as economic problems

or business ethics. He would argue that these are too ancillary to the main question at hand: an exposition of what it means to be Christian.

Before addressing the moral questions concerning sex and marriage, Lewis stops to make some observations about psychoanalysis. He accepts the Freudian techniques of psychoanalysis while rejecting the Freudian materialistic psychology, preferring the interpretations of Jung to Freud. One must not confuse the making of moral choices with the psychological therapy which may be necessary to help clarify those choices. All of us may have psychological "hang-ups" of one kind or another which color our behaviour; we are not justified or condemned by our psychological conditioning, but we are judged on the moral choices that we make. From this standpoint, the retarded, the manic-depressive, the sick, the disadvantaged, the schizophrenic all become judged as morally responsible agents. People judge us by our external actions, but God judges the heart and will reward or punish us on the basis of how well we have used the talents he has given us. Lewis thinks there will be some surprises in store for all of us.

Before sexual morality can be discussed meaningfully, a distinction must be made between *chastity* and *propriety*. Dress today is considerably more casual than it was in Victorian times, yet clothes or the absence of clothes do not necessarily reflect on a person's chastity (or unchastity). What Lewis says is that *how* something is worn is more important than *what* is worn, and he extended this principle into the complicated field of pornography in an article entitled "Prudery and Philology" (*The Spectator*, 21 January 1955). It is the manner or way in which something is presented to us, with or without the intention of inflaming our passions, rather than *what* is presented that makes it objectionable or not. The same principle might well be applied to the controversial subject of violence in the movies or on television.

Chastity is the most unpopular of the Christian virtues because it demands either marriage with complete faithfulness to one's partner or total abstinence. But this is quite contrary to our fallen natures; so either Christianity is too harsh in its demands or our sexual natures in their present state have badly gone astray. In a celebrated passage in "Christian Behaviour," Lewis writes:

> You can get a large audience together for a strip-tease act—that is, to watch a girl undress on the stage. Now suppose you came to a country where you could fill a theatre by simply bringing a covered plate on to the stage and then slowly lifting the cover so as to let every one see, just before the lights went out, that it contained a mutton chop or a bit of bacon, would you not think that in that country something had gone wrong with the appetite for food? And would not anyone who had grown up in a different world think there was something equally queer about the state of the sex instinct among us?[17]

Someone may argue that such behavior is an indication of sexual starvation, but the facts of the matter indicate that there is a good deal of sexual activity taking place all around. Instead of starvation, it may be a case of gluttony! Against the charge that sex is in a mess because it has been hushed up, Lewis argues just the opposite: that sex has been over-publicized. Against the argument that sex is nothing to be ashamed of, he distinguishes between the sexual instinct itself which he believes to be good (created by God) and the sexual instinct's present day corruption into all sorts of vices, which he deems obviously bad. A civilization which emphasized food out of all proper proportion would be just as perverse as one which idolized sex.

In an article entitled "We Have No 'Right to Happiness' " (contained in *God in the Dock*), Lewis explains why the sex instinct above all others seems to be out of control. Suffice it to say that our warped natures, the temptations of demons and all the contemporary propaganda for lust "combine to make us feel that the desires we are resisting are so 'natural,' so 'healthy,' and so reasonable, that it is almost perverse and abnormal to resist them."[18]

But they must be resisted, and with God's help they can be resisted successfully. Restraint is necessary if any kind of happiness is to be achieved in this world, because indulgence of all the passions will lead to the destruction of the individual. I think discipline is a better word than restraint, which immediately suggests the notion of repression or driving some desire into the subconscious. To resist a conscious desire is "suppression" and can lead to a good knowledge of one's own sexuality. Suppression brings virtue: indulgence creates a fog.

It is only in Christian marriage that sexual intercourse finds its proper use. The whole doctrine of Christian marriage is based on Christ's words that man and woman were made for each other, that the two were to become one flesh. The oneness in marriage extends not merely to sex but to every aspect of the union of two people. Adultery and fornication are monstrous because they try to separate the sexual aspect of union from all others. Marriage is for life; all churches consider divorce a serious business, whether they prohibit it or allow it in exceptional cases. Holy matrimony is until "death do us part," with promises made before God "and this company." These promises are easy to keep when one is "in love," but initial infatuation is only a temporary state for most people; the promises must be kept even after one has passed this first stage. Marriage promises provide a home for the children and protect the woman, who may have sacrificed a career, from being dropped on the whim of the man.

One of the recurrent themes in all of Lewis's writings is the warning against trying to recapture or repeat pleasures or thrills. This applies to "being in love." Infatuation is wonderful for the young, but it was never meant to last. It is like the explosion that starts the locomotive down the matrimonial track. When people find later that they no longer possess this great passion, they imagine that they have married the wrong person, and may seek to break up the matrimonial tie. This is a mistake, because when a new love comes down the pike, that may prove to be no more lasting than the first love. What should happen is that new interests, new surprises, new thrills present themselves as we advance in life. Unfortunately, the wrong kind of pulp magazines, movies, and television shows mislead us by glamorizing romance and tricking us into thinking that infatuations last forever. They don't. They were not meant to.

Connected with the idea of divorce is the notion that falling in love with somebody else is irresistible. What Lewis should say is that attractions can be stopped at some point along the line; we do have control over our emotions, at least at the beginning of a relationship. Disasters occur later because the will was not exercised soon enough. Much grief could be spared. Lewis does not say it, but he might have observed that many defections from the priesthood could likewise be stopped if precautions had been taken in sufficient time. Again, it is a question of exercising the will and asking for God's grace to persevere in one's first commitment.

Lewis would like to distinguish between two kinds of marriage: Christian marriage and state or secular marriage. Since most people are not Christians, the state should make rules which would be binding on all citizens, while the Church would have rules enforced on her own members. And it ought to be clear to everybody who is married in the secular and who is married in the Christian sense. But what does this mean? Would divorce be easier in the secular sense? And does this not open the door to a kind of ethical relativism, which Lewis has taken great pains to refute? Lewis does not spell out what he means by this brief but tantalizing suggestion. It may be just as well.

While it would be wrong and misleading to suggest that Lewis is no friend of women, he does hold that the man is the proper head of the household, and that in some instances the woman must defer to him when a serious argument cannot be resolved in any other way. This particular bit of Lewisiana has excited no end of scorn, but it nevertheless has Pauline roots. Lewis holds that some kind of headship is necessary if the marriage is to be permanent. And he holds that this must be vested in the man because most women (and presumably all men) want it that way. Men are apt to be more rational and less emotional than women; they are apt to be fairer in the family's "foreign policy" (how it deals with the outside world); and women do not respect men who allow themselves to be dominated. Now, all of this may sound like male chauvinism in this present day, but Lewis's reply to his attackers would be: "Look closely at the facts and see if I'm not right."

Finally, with regard to sex, what is his attitude toward homosexuality? To a Benedictine monk in England, Lewis writes:

> The stories you tell about the two perverts belong to a terribly familiar pattern: the man of good will, saddled with an abnormal desire wh. he never chose, fighting hard and time after time defeated. But I question whether in such a life the successful operation of Grace is so tiny as we think. Is not this continued avoidance either of presumption or despair, this ever renewed struggle itself a great triumph of Grace? Perhaps more so than the (to human eyes) equable virtue of some who are psychologically sound.[19]

Here he acknowledges that abnormal desires may be thrust upon a person; one does not choose them. We have already seen that Lewis had had ample opportunity at Malvern College to witness life as lived by the "Bloods" and the "Tarts," although his brother Warren says he exaggerated this. In *Surprised by Joy*, Lewis comments that he was never tempted to this vice; the fact is that it all rather bored him.[20]

"Jack" Lewis was a man of great compassion. On 1 February 1958 he wrote to Mrs. Edward A. Allen:

> I quite agree with the Archbishop that no *sin*, simply as such, should be made a *crime*. Who the deuce are our rulers to enforce their opin-

ions about sin on us?—a lot of professional politicians, often venal
time-servers, whose opinion on a moral problem in one's own life we
shd. attach very little value to. Of course many acts which are sins
against God are also injuries to our fellow-citizens, and must on that
account, but only on that account, be made crimes. But of all the sins
in the world I shd. have thought homosexuality was the one that least
concerns the State. We hear too much of the State. Government is at
its best a necessary evil. Let's keep it in its place.[21]

In addition to a very tolerant attitude toward homosexuality, Lewis
reveals his political theory that the best government is the one
which governs least. His attitude toward politicians is simply a
personal bias.

Again, to Delmar Banner he wrote two years later,

I'm glad you liked the book [*The Four Loves*]. I quite agree with
you about homosexuals; to make the thing criminal cures nothing and
only creates a blackmailer's paradise. . . . But I couldn't well have a
digression on that. One is fighting on two fronts, (a) for the perse-
cuted homo *against* the widespread freemasonry of the high-brow
homos who dominate so much of the world of criticism and won't be
v. nice to you unless you are in their set. . . .[22]

While sympathetic to the problem and opposed to governmental
snooping, here he is equally opposed to the officious exclusiveness
of certain high-brow literati. In fact, they may have helped to in-
spire his sermon entitled "The Inner Ring."

In *The Four Loves*, the discussion revolves around affection,
friendship, erotic love and the love of God. In the chapter on
friendship, Lewis asks whether every firm and serious friendship
is really homosexual. The fact that no positive evidence of homosexuality can be discovered in the behavior of two friends does
not mean, say the "wiseacres," that it is not *really* there. In this
case, the word *really* means hidden or subconsciously. But in this
situation, the very lack of proof is taken for proof. Lewis asserts
that those who cannot conceive of friendship as a substantive love,
but only as a disguise or elaboration of eros, betray the fact that

they have never had a friend. He does not even think that the homosexual theory is plausible. Admitting that in certain instances friendship and abnormal eros can be combined, and that in certain social situations (military, jail, etc.) where there is an absence of the opposite sex it may be combined, Lewis believes that it is actually the absence of demonstrative gestures in our own society which demands some explanation. The modern world which sees homosexual overtones in every demonstration of affection is actually the society which is out of step.[23]

In *The Problem of Pain* Lewis devotes two chapters to the discussion of human pain, and indirectly refers to those who have to bear the pain of a "loathsome disease." He is not referring specifically to homosexuality so much as to any burden which must be borne by someone who has not chosen this particular cross to carry. It is in the eyes of society that certain "diseases" can be loathsome, and for all of the progress in tolerance during the past few years, there are still many areas of society which look at homosexuality as something quite repulsive. The point Lewis is making here is that many who carry heavy crosses are especially close to God, and loneliness involved in such suffering will be generously rewarded and can have enormous intercessory value. Dom Aelred Watkin says much the same thing about unrequited love in his splendid little book *The Enemies of Love*.

But all of this must be placed against the larger background of sexual ethic, of which homosexuality is only a part for Lewis. Christianity insists that only two life styles are possible: either monogamy or, outside of marriage, complete sexual abstinence. This may seem narrow and exclusive, but it is patently clear in the Jewish-Christian tradition. Nor can the Church or the Synagogue be faulted in this respect; the quarrel is with their founders. The modern world certainly does not preach either continence or chastity, but perhaps no society has ever done so in actuality. Lewis feels the only life style which will really succeed is the chaste one. Abstinence brings freedom, joy, and inner peace, and ultimately enables one to be a true son of God. Sexual license, he asserts, will produce only misery, unhappiness and self-hatred, and in the final analysis one becomes an everlasting horror to one's self.

Lewis was not a pacifist. He served in France in the Somerset Light Infantry during World War I, was wounded, was decorated for assisting in the surrender of some sixty German prisoners of war, and was honorably discharged. During World War II, he was active on the home front. In his opinion it is perfectly right for a Christian judge to sentence a man to death or a Christian soldier to kill an enemy. But it is the manner in which this is done which is most important. One must kill without hatred, and one must forgive one's enemies. The New Testament says we are not to murder, there being a sharp distinction between killing and murdering. In "Christian Behaviour," Lewis puts it succinctly:

> All killing is not murder any more than all sexual intercourse is adultery. When soldiers came to St. John the Baptist asking what to do, he never remotely suggested that they ought to leave the army; nor did Christ when He met a Roman sergeant-major—what they called a centurion. The idea of the knight—the Christian in arms for the defence of a good cause—is one of the great Christian ideas. War is a dreadful thing, and I can respect an honest pacifist, though I think he is entirely mistaken. What I cannot understand is this sort of semi-pacifism you get nowadays which gives people the idea that though you have to fight, you ought to do it with a long face and as if you were ashamed of it. It is that feeling that robs lots of magnificent young Christians in the Services of something they have a right to, something which is the natural accompaniment of courage—a kind of gaity and wholeheartedness.[24]

This was written during war time, and in rejecting both pacifism and the Augustinian "just but mournful war" Lewis is left with little else but the crusading idea. Nor is his New Testament exegesis very sound in trying to conclude something that Christ did not tell the centurion to do. Also, the early Church was pacifist for the very cogent reason that the state was persecuting the new religion. Bad as war can be, there are still some things which are worse. It may be hard for a Pole or a Jew to forgive the Gestapo, but Christ's terrible words are that if we fail to forgive, God will not forgive us. So we are left with one of the most unpopular of the Christian virtues: the necessity of forgiving our enemies.

Writing later on Pacifism, Lewis states: "This, then, is why I am not a Pacifist. If I tried to become one, I should find a very doubtful factual basis, an obscure train of reasoning, a weight of authority both human and Divine against me, and strong grounds for suspecting that my wishes had directed my decision. As I have said, moral decisions do not admit of mathematical certainty. It may be, after all, that Pacifism is right. But it seems to me very long odds, longer odds than I would care to take with the voice of almost all humanity against me."[25]

In *The Screwtape Letters* it is instructive to examine how the devils view the humans' war; do wars work to his Satanic Majesty's advantage or not? Screwtape writes:

> Of course a war is entertaining. The immediate fear and suffering of the humans is a legitimate and pleasing refreshment for our myriads of toiling workers. But what permanent good does it do us unless we make use of it for bringing souls to Our Father Below?. . . . Let us therefore think rather how to use, than how to enjoy, this European war. For it has certain tendencies inherent in it which are, in themselves, by no means in our favour. We may hope for a good deal of cruelty and unchastity. But, if we are not careful, we shall see thousands turning in this tribulation to the Enemy, while tens of thousands who do not go so far as that will nevertheless have their attention diverted from themselves to values and causes which they believe to be higher than the self.[26]

War turns out to be ambivalent. It is not a good, but it is not an unmitigated evil either. However, in World War II the issues seemed fairly black and white. Lewis would say that, like everything else, wars must be judged on whether they move the "patient" toward the Enemy (God) or toward the infernal regions of Our Father Below.

At the beginning of this chapter, we alluded to the fact that Lewis does have a philosophy of history. Essentially, he holds the Augustinian concept of the two cities which continue to grow until the end of the world. In the space trilogy we are told that the silent planet (earth) will soon be invaded by forces for good and finally by Maleldil (God) himself. Then evil will be shown for what it is, and the world will be cleansed. The idea that earth is enemy-occupied territory which God will one day "invade" appears again in *Mere Christianity*, and the Day of Judgment is quite clearly depicted in *The Last Battle*.

Lewis's ethic is highly individualistic and highly personal. This is not to say that he is opposed to social service, social action or social programs for the betterment of the human race. But the radical evil which lies at the heart of society is due primarily to personal sin. Society is corrupt because individuals are corrupt. Of course it is true that immoral society may corrupt moral individuals, but for Lewis most social ills are individual ills writ large. Erase the effects of original and personal sin, and the world will become as God intended it. Society will improve only when persons undergo genuine conversion experiences which result in deep personal commitments.

The Last Things

Human death is a result of human sin. When he was first created, man was immune from death, and when he is finally redeemed and called to a new life, he will be immune from death once again. Throughout his writings, but especially in *Miracles*, Lewis insists that man is a composite being. Naturalism refutes itself because man cannot be explained solely in naturalistic terms; he has a mind which clearly transcends nature and can even modify and control nature. That man is nothing but a natural organism is disproved by the fact that man thinks rational thoughts which could never be produced by irrational nature. Certainly man has a physical body which is part of nature, but he also has a supernatural spirit. Ideally the two should form a symbiotic relationship.

At present, however, these two principles in man are not on the best of terms. The natural man is in a state or process of steady disintegration that ultimately results in death. The spiritual aspect of man attempts to retain its foothold against the constant counterattacks of nature (both physiological and psychological), only to be defeated in the end. But, Lewis tells us, Christianity holds that this was not always so. At one time the spirit was fully at home with its organism and the two seemed made for each other, like horse and rider or king and country—or perhaps like the mythical centaur whose human part was at home with his equine part. When this situation existed—when the organism did not rebel—death did not occur.

But now man's nature rebels constantly. And when it dominates spirit, it wrecks all spiritual activities (and itself as well). Spirit, on the other hand, confirms and improves natural activities when it is able to dominate nature. Thus the reasonable and virtuous man has a better body (other beings being equal) than the foolish or debauched man. Christianity, says Lewis, tells us that this rebellion of the lower nature had a beginning in time and will also have a conclusion at some future date. It began with primal man's first disobedience, which brought upon him the necessity for work, pain, grief and finally death. Eventually there will be a reconciliation; indeed a reconciliation is already taking place.

The fact that this discomfort between the supernatural spirit and the natural organism in man did not always exist, that it is an unnatural state, can be confirmed by examining two aspects of human behavior. The first is the tendency to make "coarse jokes." This illustrates how ill at ease people can be with their bodies; they find their animality either objectionable or funny. Dogs do not find dogs funny, and in all likelihood angels do not find angels funny. The second proof rests in our feeling about the dead: we find them uncanny. We dislike corpses; we fear ghosts. We feel that the human person ought not to be divided, and death makes the division particularly evident to us. It is useless to resort to a doctrine of primitive superstitions and taboos to explain our present feelings, for obviously these are the results, not the causes, of our feelings. Only the Christian doctrine, which asserts that man was originally a unity and the present division is unnatural, adequately explains the phenomena.[1]

"If there is any thought at which a Christian trembles, it is the thought of God's 'judgment.' The 'Day' of Judgement is 'that day of wrath, that dreadful day.' We pray to God to deliver us 'in the hour of death and at the day of judgement.' "[2] Long expressed in Christian art and music, the terrors of the day of judgment come to quintessential expression in the Dies Irae. This teaching clearly comes from Jesus himself, and is illustrated by the frightening parable of the sheep and the goats. What is particularly appalling is the fact that the goats are condemned on the grounds of what they have not done. It is our sins of omission which damn us. Worse, we may be damned for things which we never dreamed of doing. Still worse, the judgment takes place against impossible standards which no one can hope or expect to meet. The Judge is the Spotless One, and since sin is a heinous offence in God's eyes, all are worthy of condemnation. So let there be no talk of merits, says Lewis; here it is a question of throwing one's self on the mercy of God and relying only on the merits of Christ.

But there is a Jewish conception of judgment which needs to be added to the Christian conception. The Jews thought of God's judgment as an earthly court of justice. The Psalmist thinks of the day of judgment as one of gladness; it is the day when finally justice will be done. The poor woman who has had her land taken away from her by a rich, more powerful neighbor will receive justice in court because at last her case will be heard. Many people would be vindicated if they could only get their case into court. When God finally comes to judge the earth, this will be a day of victory for those people.

The issues upon which judgment hangs are heaven or hell; yet Lewis believes in purgatory. Applauding the reformers for rejecting the degraded notion of purgatory which had developed in the sixteenth century (his condemnation is superficial and based on a few excessive sermons of the period) and recalling that purgatory, after all, is a vestibule of heaven, Lewis says in a delightful passage: "Our souls *demand* purgatory, don't they? Would it not break the heart if God said to us, 'It is true, my son, that your breath smells and your rags drip with mud and slime, but we are charitable here and no one will upbraid you with these things, nor draw away from you. Enter into the joy'? Should we not reply, 'With submission, sir, and if there is no objection, I'd *rather* be cleaned first.' 'It may hurt, you know'—'even so, sir.' "[3]

It seems obvious that the process of purification will involve suffering, but the purpose of the purification would involve that only indirectly. Nor can one say how much cleansing may be necessary; the treatment given will be the one required, whether it hurts much or little. Lewis wisely does not commit himself as to whether or not there is fire in purgatory, a point which has been left an open matter by the Latin church. And if we take the following illustration literally, he clearly does not think there is: "My favorite image on this matter comes from the dentist's chair. I hope that when the tooth of life is drawn and I am 'coming around,' a voice will say, 'Rinse your mouth out with this.' This will be a purgatory."[4]

The major thing Lewis does is to establish the logical necessity for purgatory, which Protestantism (he feels) has unfortunately discarded. But that does not automatically put Lewis in the Catholic camp (that's why he saluted the sixteenth century reformers). Always his point of view is that of "mere Christianity," a halfway position which we have already tried to show is untenable.

When and how will the end come? If we are speaking of our own human lives, we can say that the end will probably come without warning. "You know not the day or the hour." If we are speaking of the end of the world, that also will come without warning. Lewis reminds us that we have no idea what part of the play we are in, whether it is act 1 or act 5. We do not even know who the major or minor characters are. We cannot see the play as a whole. The best we can do is to play our part when we are on stage, and to play it as well as possible. Only the Author is thoroughly acquainted with both the past and the future. We too may find out when it is over, but we can be sure of one thing: the Author will comment on our performance, whether it was badly executed or well played. The playing of our role well is what is infinitely important.[5]

Lewis illustrates this point with a passage from *King Lear*. In act 3 old Gloucester is being blinded, and at this outrage the "first servant" draws his sword and points it at his master's breast. It is of no use; Regan stabs him from behind. The scene is very brief, eight lines in all, but Lewis declares that this servant's role is the noblest one in the entire play. When the curtain goes down on act 5, this part is the one which would have been most pleasing in God's eyes.

With regard to hell, the Oxford don has written much. It is certainly an important element in *The Screwtape Letters* and mentions of it are scattered throughout his other writings. But his position is stated most clearly and convincingly in *The Problem of Pain*, and indeed chapter 8 is devoted to the subject of hell. Lewis calls hell the *intolerable doctrine*, and he proceeds to deal with the major objections that moderns raise with regard to it. He does not intend to prove the doctrine tolerable; it is *not* tolerable. He proposes merely to respond to some objections people have concerning hell.

The first objection is the idea of retributive punishment as such. Take, for example, a man who is absolutely immoral. Suppose he reaches a position of power through purely selfish means, and has violated all the canons of honesty and decency along the way. He laughs at the noble emotions of his victims and uses his pinnacle position to gratify every conceivable lust, hatred and cruelty. He even betrays his own benefactors and accomplices at the end, loudly proclaiming that there is no God, and that all men are fools. Even death finds him unrepentant. Are we to say that justice should still be thwarted, and that infinite mercy should be extended to a man who does not even consider that he needs forgiveness? That would be to give the lie to the entire universe, for surely at some point this man must know that he is evil, and also that his evil life has been contrary to his very nature. To deny that this monster should ever be brought to final justice is to deny that God and his justice exist, or that this is a moral universe. And such a conclusion would have to be intolerable.

A second objection turns on the seeming inequity of punishing transitory sin with eternal damnation. But Lewis points out that we do not have a very adequate understanding of what time itself is, nor should we regard eternity as merely endless time. Our human understanding of time is linear, one event follows another, but in eternity time may have thickness as well as length, and indeed the greater reality beyond death may be thought of as three or even multi-dimensional. Admittedly this is hard to picture, but conceivably what we understand as time in this world may be something quite different in the hereafter.

A third objection turns on the frightful intensity of the pains of hell. Jesus generally speaks of hell as a place of punishment, or of destruction, or of privation. In Matthew 25:46 those who have failed to do corporal works of mercy are to depart into everlasting torment. Our Lord wishes to portray something unspeakably horrible. In Matthew 10:28 we are told to fear him who is able to destroy both body and soul in hell. But the worst punishment of all seems to be that of banishment. Those thrust into outward darkness presumably never see the divine light again. Weeping, wailing and gnashing of teeth characterize remorse. Privation seems to be essentially a spiritual punishment which is more grievous than any physical agony. It would of course be more pleasant to speak of the annihilation of the soul, and this is theoretically possible. But this is not the way God acts. Lewis uses the illustration of a burning log which is changed into heat, gas and ashes. There is such a thing as having been a log, even though what remains after burning is only useless residue. Similarly, there must be such a thing as having been a soul!

A further objection to hell is that no blessed person in heaven could be happy if he or she knew that some person (perhaps only one person) were suffering in hell. But Lewis thinks that Our Lord does not stress the temporal duration of the suffering in hell so much as he stresses the finality of the story. Certainly the lost soul is fixed in its diabolical hatred, but Lewis thinks we cannot say whether this eternal fixity implies endless duration, or duration at all. But here I think Lewis misreads the Gospel; granted the notion of fixity, the notion of duration is suggested by the "worm which dies not and the fire which is not quenched." Again, the whole problem may hang on the notion of time and whether there is a linear time in hell which parallels that on earth (Dante seems to imply this) or whether other states of being have their own time, or indeed no time at all.

A final objection to hell is that the loss of a single soul implies failure on the part of God. But one must remember that God creates souls with free wills, and free will means that the creature may resist God to the very end. Even though hell is a horrible torment to the damned, still heaven would be a worse torment. God never violates free will; this the damned retain to the very end. So in a sense we can say that hell is locked on the inside; the damned may wish they were not there, but they do not wish to come out. Encountering the divine Love would be a worse torture than they now endure.

The entire matter is beautifully summarized in a few lines from *The Problem of Pain*: "In the long run the answer to all those who object to the doctrine of hell, is itself a question: 'What are you asking God to do?' To wipe out their past sins and, at all costs, to give them a fresh start, smoothing every difficulty and offering every miraculous help? But He has done so, on Calvary. To forgive them? They will not be forgiven. To leave them alone? Alas, I am afraid that is what He does."[6]

The Screwtape Letters offer us a picture of hell, not from the human but the demonic point of view. The aim of the tempters is to gain food for themselves from the damned souls whose free will has brought them finally to the miserific vision. Screwtape writes: "If . . . by steady and cool-headed application here and now you can finally secure his soul, he will then be yours forever—a brimfull living chalice of despair and horror and astonishment which you can raise to your lips as often as you please."[7] Hell affords a peculiar kind of clarity; one "patient" said on his arrival there, "I now see that I spent most of my life in doing *neither* what I ought *nor* what I liked."[8] And this particular letter ends with some of Lewis's most often quoted lines: "You will say that these are very small sins; and doubtless, like all young tempters, you are anxious to be able to report spectacular wickedness. But do remember, the only thing that matters is the extent to which you separate the man from the Enemy. It does not matter how small the sins are, provided that their cumulative effect is to edge the man away from the Light and out into the Nothing."[9]

Whatever else hell may be, it is not quiet. As Screwtape tells us, "No square inch of infernal space and no moment of infernal time has been surrendered to either of those abominable forces [music and silence], but all has been occupied by Noise—Noise, the grand dynamism, the audible expression of all that is exultant, ruthless and virile—Noise which alone defends us from silly qualms, despairing scruples, and impossible desires. We will make the whole universe a noise in the end."[10] Lewis might have added (I'm not sure he ever mentions it) that hell is one fetid stench. All of the senses are revolted by hell, and certainly the senses of smell and taste. Somewhere Lewis does mention fragrances as being characteristic of heaven, but hell presents us with the olefactory "delights" of putrid putrescence.

Lewis has a good deal to say about hell in his writings, not because he is drawn to a fascination with the lurid, nor because of any morbid sense, but because he feels that moderns have pretty largely discarded this belief. How they could have in view of the history of the twentieth century is beyond imagination, but Lewis believes that it is the contemporary strategy of hell to hide itself. Because we find the picture of a devil in red tights (on the side of an Underwood can of deviled ham) amusing, and cannot take that seriously, we find it impossible to take seriously the reality of any devils. Science has helped to do away with a belief in devils, and although all the evidence is to the contrary, modern man prefers to relegate these noxious beings to medieval times.

In *The Great Divorce*, Lewis describes hell as the "grey town," where there is a perpetual twilight and drizzling rain. It is a town of dingy lodging houses, small tobacconists, hoardings (billboards) from which posters hang in rags, windowless warehouses, goods stations without trains, and bookshops of the sort that sell *The Works of Aristotle*. Parts of it are quite empty because the neighbors are in the habit of quarrelling with one another, and it is possible to move one's residence simply by thinking of a new house on the edge of town, thus leaving more and more empty streets. The older inhabitants of hell live millions of miles away, and millions of miles from one another. We learn that the population is all ghostly; in fact, when the busload of ghosts arrives in heaven, they find that the solidity of reality is intolerable.

At the end of *The Great Divorce* Lewis meets his Scottish mentor George MacDonald, who warns him against being sorry for those who are in hell. It is not an infinite, empty town as previously thought, but only a small crack in heaven's ground. MacDonald says, "All Hell is smaller than one pebble of your earthly world: but it is smaller than one atom of *this* world, the Real World. Look at yon butterfly. If it swallowed all Hell, Hell would not be big enough to do it any harm or to have any taste."[11] All of Hell's miseries could be swallowed up without trace like a drop of water falling into the Pacific Ocean. It is as close to nothingness as one can get.

Lewis has as much to say about heaven as he does about hell. The reasons are similar: the aim of the spiritual life has largely been forgotten and people aren't taking seriously Saint Paul's statement that the sufferings of the present time are not worthy to be compared with the glory to come that will be revealed in us (Rom. 8:18). Moreover, it is somewhat difficult to extrapolate what heaven may be like from our earthly personal experience. Unfortunately, in the case of hell it seems to be easier!

Although references to heaven are scattered throughout Lewis's writings, the chapter entitled "Heaven" in *The Problem of Pain* gives a good overview of his thought on the subject. We are shy in speaking of heaven, he says, because this may seem like a "copout," an excuse for not addressing ourselves to pressing problems here on earth. There is also the Marxist jeer that Christians talk about "eating pie in the sky bye and bye." Lewis insists that there is either pie in the sky or there is not. If there is not, Christianity is a fraud; if there is, this fact must be faced like all other facts. Nor must we look upon heaven as a bribe for good behavior. Jesus speaks quite frankly about reward, including material reward, but the best reward is heavenly and spiritual. This rules out any mercenary idea of the Kingdom of Heaven.[12]

Do we really desire heaven? Sometimes it would seem not, but one of Lewis's favorite themes is that we have never desired anything else. This notion of yearning for we know not what—of *Sehnsucht*—forms the basis of *The Pilgrim's Regress*. It is John's longing for the purple mountains which sets him out on his spiritual quest. To be sure, this basic desire which is in every person sometimes becomes confused; it is sometimes thought to be a desire for sex, worldly advance, or power for instance. Some say it is even a hopeless delusion, impossible of fulfillment; but eventually this in-born yearning, this longing *is* fulfilled—with overwhelming joy. "Our hearts are restless until they find their rest in thee," is proven once again to be true. The *Sehnsucht* is there because we are made for heaven.

> You have never *had* it. All the things that have ever deeply possessed your soul have been but hints of it—tantalising glimpses, promises never quite fulfilled, echoes that died away just as they caught your ear. But if it should really become manifest—if there ever came an echo that did not die away but swelled into the sound itself—you would know it. Beyond all possibility of doubt you would say "Here at last is the thing I was made for." We cannot tell each other about it. It is the secret signature of each soul, the incommunicable and unappeasable want, the thing we desired . . . and which we shall still desire on our deathbeds. . . .[13]

This secret signature on each soul is unique; it is absolutely different from any other in the entire universe. It alone can answer to some special contour in the divine substance; it alone is the key that can unlock the particular mansion which corresponds to it. If we let God have his way with us in this earthly life, he will grant us complete satisfaction in the heavenly life—for after all he is our first love. Our eyes shall behold him as he is, blessed and fortunate creatures that we are. Our places in heaven will seem to be made for us, and for us alone, because God has been preparing each one "stitch by stitch as a glove is made for a hand."[14]

The thing we long for summons us out of ourselves. Yet we cannot concentrate on it or else it will elude us; it comes to us in our unguarded moments, unsuspectingly. It is like the fragrance of unseen roses; the only cure for this *Sehnsucht* is work. Like happiness it cannot be sought directly; it is a byproduct of the daily scene. The satisfaction always refuses to be present when most expected.

In heaven there is no ownership; all things are held in common. And yet, "To him that overcometh I will give a white stone, and in the stone a new name written, which no man knoweth saving he that receiveth it" (Rev. 2:17). Lewis interprets this to mean that each one of the redeemed will forever know and praise some one aspect of the divine beauty better than any other creature can praise it. Although God is utterly simple, he produces infinite variety in each of his effects, and every soul differs from every other soul so that no two render identical worship. What results is a celestial harmony of infinite variety.[15]

Lewis might have said that in hell there are tables groaning with food, and seated at the tables are those who would indeed satisfy their hunger, but they cannot because their elbows are locked. They cannot bend their arms, so that in spite of the feast those in hell must starve. In heaven also there are tables groaning with food, and likewise there are those seated at the tables who would satisfy their hunger, although their elbows too are locked and they cannot bend their arms. But they do not starve in heaven; they have learned to feed each other.

Lewis concludes his discussion of heaven in *The Problem of Pain* with another of his favorite themes, the idea of the *cosmic dance*. "All pains and pleasures we have known on earth are early initiations in the movements of that dance: but the dance itself is strictly incomparable with the sufferings of this present time. As we draw nearer to its uncreated rhythm, pain and pleasure sink almost out of sight. There is joy in the dance, but it does not exist for the sake of joy. It does not even exist for the sake of good, or of love. It is Love Himself, and Good Himself, and therefore happy. It does not exist for us, but we for it."[16]

A parallel idea less clearly spelled out is the idea of the *cosmic game*, whose first rule is that every player must by all means touch the ball and then immediately pass it on. To be found with the ball in your hands is a fault, to cling to it is death. The ball flies swiftly to and fro among the players while the great Master himself leads the revelry, giving himself eternally to his creatures in the generation, and back to himself in the sacrifice, of the Word.[17] This idea of the *cosmic game* is just suggested by Lewis. (Remember, he detested games of any kind).

It is fitting that *The Chronicles of Narnia* should conclude on a "heavenly" note, for at the end of *The Last Battle* there is a destruction of the old universe, and the restoration of the new Narnia. Surprise follows surprise to delight the Pevensie children as they are bidden to go "further up and further in." And this is only the beginning of the real story. "All their life in this world and all their adventures in Narnia," says Lewis, "had only been the cover and the title page."[18]

But the most spectacular and moving bit of writing about heaven comes at the end of *The Screwtape Letters*. In the last letter, the "hero" or patient about whom Wormwood and Screwtape have been writing, is killed in an air raid. His trial is over and he faces the heavenly Persons. Screwtape rebukes Wormwood for allowing a Christian to slip from his grasp. Screwtape describes the end:

> As he saw you, he also saw Them. . . . He had no faintest conception till that very hour of how they would look, and even doubted their existence. But when he saw them he knew that he had always known them and realised what part each one of them had played at many an hour in his life when he had supposed himself alone, so that now he could say to them, one by one, not "Who *are* you?" but "So it was you all the time."

> He saw not only Them; he saw Him. This animal, this thing begotten in a bed, could look on Him. What is blinding, suffocating fire to you, is now cool light to him, is clarity itself, and wears the form of a

Man. You would like, if you could, to interpret the patient's prostra-
tion in the Presence, his self-abhorrence and utter knowledge of his
sins (yes, Wormwood, a clearer knowledge even than yours) on the
analogy of your own choking and paralysing sensations when you encounter the deadly air that breathes from the heart of Heaven. But it's
all nonsense. Pains he may still have to encounter, but they *embrace*
those pains. They would not barter them for any earthly pleasure. All
the delights of sense, or heart, or intellect, with which you could once
have tempted him, even the delights of virtue itself, now seem to him
in comparison but as the half nauseous attractions of a raddled harlot
would seem to a man who hears that his true beloved whom he has
loved all his life and whom he had believed to be dead is alive and
even now at his door. He is caught up into that world where pain and
pleasure take on transfinite values.[19]

This is Lewis at his finest. Any additional comment would be
superfluous. Suffice it to say that Lewis's keen sense of the goals
of the spiritual life enable him to give a sure-footed direction to
the subordinate ends of that life as well.

In his essay "The World's Last Night," Lewis recalls to our
minds that Christ's Second Coming is also a major ingredient in
the Gospel message. For various reasons Lewis feels that the fact
that "He shall come to judge the living and the dead" has been
soft-pedaled in the twentieth century. It is not so. Lewis ignores
the large number of Adventists, Jehovah's Witnesses, Pentecostals
and others for whom this is a key point. A cursory look at the
world scene lends credence to their conviction. What Lewis stresses
is that the Second Coming will occur with absolutely no warning
whatever. The very best preparation for it is not to be caught off
guard. In spite of the apocalyptic interpretations of the school of
Albert Schweitzer, not even the Son himself knows when the end
of the world is coming. All are to watch, to be constantly prepared, lest their house be broken into when they are not looking.

One can call Lewis the "master of the grand finale." This tele-
ological spirituality (reminiscent of Erigena) sets the whole

raison d'etre for Christianity and needs to be firmly rooted in the consciousness of the twentieth century. Nowhere is Lewis ever more eloquent or convincing than when writing about "The Last Things."

Notes

CHAPTER 1   The Reluctant Convert

1. C. S. Lewis, *Surprised by Joy: The Shape of My Early Life* (New York: Harcourt Brace Jovanovich, 1955), chap. 1, p. 10.

2. W. H. Lewis, *Letters of C. S. Lewis* (New York: Harcourt, Brace & World, Inc., 1966), p. 2.

3. Lewis, *Surprised by Joy*, chap. 2, pp. 33–34.

4. Ibid., chap. 3, p. 53.

5. W. H. Lewis, *Letters of C. S. Lewis*, pp. 4–5.

6. Walter Hooper, ed., *They Stand Together: The Letters of C. S. Lewis to Arthur Greeves, 1914–1963* (New York: Macmillan Publishing Co., Inc., 1979).

7. Lewis, *Surprised by Joy*, chap. 9, p. 133.

8. Ibid., chap. 12, p. 188.

9. Roger Lancelyn Green and Walter Hooper, *C. S. Lewis: A Biography* (New York: Harcourt Brace Jovanovich, 1974), chap. 2, p. 58.

10. Ibid., chap. 3, p. 82.

11. Lewis, *Surprised by Joy*, chap. 14, p. 220.

12. Douglas Gilbert and Clyde S. Kilby, *C. S. Lewis: Images of His World* (Grand Rapids, Mich.: Wm. B. Eerdmans Publishing Co., 1973), p. 20.

13. Lewis, *Surprised by Joy*, chap. 14, pp. 228–229.

14. Ibid., chap. 15, p. 237.

15. Gilbert and Kilby, *Images of His World*, p. 12.

16. Green and Hooper, *C. S. Lewis: A Biography*, chap. 5, pp. 132–133.

17. W. H. Lewis, *Letters of C. S. Lewis*, pp. 166–167.

18. Ibid., p. 188.

19. Green and Hooper, *C. S. Lewis: A Biography*, chap. 8, p. 196, cf. pp. 192ff.

20. Ibid., chap. 9, pp. 211–212.

21. Ibid., chap. 10, p. 256. Chapter 10 is a firsthand account of how the *Chronicles* came to be, and it contains many of Roger L. Green's personal reminiscences.

CHAPTER 2   God as God

1. C. S. Lewis, *Miracles: A Preliminary Study* (1947; reprint, New York: Macmillan Publishing Co., Inc., Macmillan Paperbacks Edition, 1978), chap. 11, pp. 87–88.

2. Ibid., p. 91.

3. Ibid., p. 89.

4. C. S. Lewis, *The Problem of Pain* (1940; reprint, New York: Macmillan Publishing Co., Inc., Macmillan Paperbacks Edition, 1962), chap. 2, p. 28.

5. Ibid., chap. 3.

6. C. S. Lewis, *That Hideous Strength: A Modern Fairy-Tale for Grown-Ups* (1945; reprint, New York: Macmillan Publishing Co., Inc., Macmillan Paperbacks Edition, 1965), chap. 15, pp. 326–327.

7. Lewis, *Problem of Pain*, chap. 10, p. 154.

8. C. S. Lewis, *Reflections on the Psalms* (New York: Harcourt Brace Jovanovich, 1958), chap. 6, p. 61.

9. C. S. Lewis, *The Four Loves* (New York: Harcourt Brace Jovanovich, 1960), chap. 6, p. 176.

10. Lewis, *Problem of Pain*, chap. 3, pp. 43–44.

11. Ibid., pp. 46–47.

12. C. S. Lewis, *Mere Christianity* (1952; reprint, New York: Macmillan Publishing Co., Inc., Macmillan Paperbacks Edition, 1960), bk. 4, chap. 4, p. 151.

13. Ibid., p. 152.

14. C. S. Lewis, *The Lion, the Witch and the Wardrobe: A Story for*

Children (1950; reprint, New York: Macmillan Publishing Co., Inc., Collier Books, 1970), chap. 8, p. 75.

15. Ibid., chap. 15, pp. 159–160.

16. C. S. Lewis, *Prince Caspian: The Return to Narnia* (1951; reprint, New York: Macmillan Publishing Co., Inc., Collier Books, 1970), chap. 10, pp. 136–138.

17. C. S. Lewis, *The Silver Chair* (1953; reprint, New York: Macmillan Publishing Co., Inc., Collier Books, 1970), chap. 10, p. 134.

18. C. S. Lewis, *The Voyage of the "Dawn Treader"* (1952; reprint, New York: Macmillan Publishing Co., Inc., Collier Books, 1970), chap. 10, p. 135.

19. C. S. Lewis, *The Horse and His Boy* (1954; reprint, New York: Macmillan Publishing Co., Inc., Collier Books, 1970), chap. 14, p. 193.

20. Ibid., chap. 11, p. 160.

21. Lewis, *Silver Chair*, chap. 2, pp. 16–17.

22. Lewis, *Voyage of the "Dawn Treader,"* chap. 7, p. 90.

23. C. S. Lewis, *The Last Battle* (1956; reprint, New York: Macmillan Publishing Co., Inc., Collier Books, 1970), chap. 13, p. 148.

24. Ibid., chap. 16, p. 184.

CHAPTER 3 God as Creator

1. Lewis, *Prince Caspian*, chap. 3, p. 28.

2. C. S. Lewis, *Out of the Silent Planet* (1938; reprint, New York: Macmillan Publishing Co., Inc., Macmillan Paperbacks Edition, 1965), chap. 18, p. 120.

3. Lewis, *Miracles*, especially chap. 2.

4. C. S. Lewis, *The Screwtape Letters* (1942; reprint, New York: Macmillan Publishing Co., Inc., 1961), letter 13, p. 59.

5. Ibid., letter 8, p. 38.

6. Ibid., letter 31, p. 146.

7. C. S. Lewis, *Perelandra: A Novel* (1943; reprint, New York: Macmil-

lan Publishing Co., Inc., Macmillan Paperbacks Edition, 1965), chap. 17, p. 212.

8. Lewis, *Screwtape Letters*, letter 1, p. 8.

9. Augustine, *Confessions*, Book 1.

10. Lewis, *Screwtape Letters*, letter 12, p. 56.

11. Lewis, *Prince Caspian*, chap. 15, pp. 211–212.

12. Ibid., chap. 9, p. 117.

13. Lewis, *Out of the Silent Planet*, chap. 12, p. 76.

14. Lewis, *Perelandra*, chap. 16, pp. 195–196.

15. Lewis, *That Hideous Strength*, chap. 7, p. 150.

CHAPTER 4   Man's Problem: Man

1. C. S. Lewis, *The Pilgrim's Regress: An Allegorical Apology for Christianity, Reason and Romanticism* (1933; reprint, New York: Bantam Books, 1981), bk. 5, chap. 2, pp. 72–74.

2. Lewis, *Screwtape Letters*, letter 19, p. 86.

3. Thomas Aquinas, *Summa Theologica*, First Part, Question 63, Article 3.

4. Lewis, *Mere Christianity*, bk. 2, pp. 53–54.

5. Lewis, *Silver Chair*, chap. 12, p. 157.

6. Ibid., pp. 161–162.

7. C. S. Lewis, *The Magician's Nephew* (1955; reprint, New York: Macmillan Publishing Co., Inc., Collier Books, 1970), chap. 13, pp. 160–161.

8. Ibid., pp. 161–162.

9. Ibid., p. 162.

10. Ibid., p. 163.

11. Ibid., p. 165.

12. Ibid., chap. 10, pp. 119–120.

13. William L. White, *The Image of Man in C. S. Lewis* (Nashville: Abingdon Press, 1969), chap. 6, p. 126.

CHAPTER 5   Jesus Christ and Redemption

1. Lewis, *Mere Christianity*, bk. 2, chap. 3, p. 52.

2. Ibid., p. 54.

3. Ibid., p. 52.

4. Ibid., p. 53.

5. Ibid., p. 55.

6. Ibid.

7. Ibid., pp. 55–56.

8. Ibid., bk. 2, chap. 5, p. 60.

9. Ibid., p. 62.

10. Ibid., p. 66.

11. Ibid., bk. 4, chap. 5, p. 157.

12. Ibid., bk. 4, chap. 9, p. 174.

13. Lewis, *That Hideous Strength*, chap. 2.

14. Lewis, *Mere Christianity*, bk. 4, chap. 10, pp. 181–182.

15. Ibid., bk. 4, chap. 11, pp. 185–187.

16. Ibid., bk. 4, chap. 10, p. 183.

CHAPTER 6   The Church and Sacraments

1. Lewis, *Screwtape Letters*, letter 1, p. 8.

2. Ibid., letter 2, p. 12.

3. Ibid.

4. Ibid., letter 7, p. 34.

5. Lewis, *Pilgrim's Regress*, bk. 5, chap. 1, pp. 70–71.

6. Ibid., bk. 5, chap. 2, pp. 72–74.

7. Ibid., bk. 7, chap. 5, p. 117.

8. Ibid., bk. 9, chap. 3, p. 172.

9. Ibid., bk. 9, chap. 4, p. 173.

10. C. S. Lewis, *Christian Reflections*, ed. Walter Hooper (Grand Rapids, Mich.: Wm. B. Eerdmans Publishing Co., 1967), p. xi.

11. Ibid., p. 166.

12. W. H. Lewis, *Letters of C. S. Lewis*, p. 170.

13. Ibid., p. 230.

14. C. S. Lewis, *Letters to Malcolm: Chiefly on Prayer* (New York: Harcourt, Brace & World, Inc., 1964), letter 19, pp. 101–102.

15. Lewis, *Mere Christianity*, bk. 3, chap. 3, p. 79.

16. Ibid., bk. 4, chap. 8, pp. 169–170.

17. C. S. Lewis, *Reflections on the Psalms* (New York: Harcourt Brace Jovanovich, 1958), chap. 12, p. 131.

18. C. S. Lewis, *The Weight of Glory and Other Addresses* (New York: The Macmillan Company, 1949), pp. 35–36.

19. James T. Como, ed., *C. S. Lewis at the Breakfast Table, and Other Reminiscences* (New York: Macmillan Publishing Co., Inc., 1979), pp. 19–20.

20. Ibid., p. 21.

21. Ibid., p. 20.

CHAPTER 7   Scripture and Prayer

1. Michael J. Christensen, *C. S. Lewis on Scripture: His Thoughts on the Nature of Biblical Inspiration, the Role of Revelation and the Question of Inerrancy* (Waco, Texas: Word Books, 1979), p. 23. Christensen is a promising young Protestant scholar who does a good job of looking at Lewis from both the conservative and liberal points of view. Fine as his study is, it would have been greatly strengthened if he had examined Catholic positions somewhat more carefully.

2. W. H. Lewis, *Letters of C. S. Lewis*, p. 286. This is from a letter written to Clyde S. Kilby on 7 May 1959.

3. Christensen, *C. S. Lewis on Scripture*, p. 97. This is from a letter written by C. S. Lewis to Corbin Carnell on 4 April 1953.

4. W. H. Lewis, *Letters of C. S. Lewis*, p. 286. From letter to C. S. Kilby cited in note 2.

5. Lewis, *Christian Reflections*, pp. 154–155, 159.

6. Ibid., p. 154.

7. Lewis, *Pilgrim's Regress*, bk. 9, chap. 5, p. 176.

8. C. S. Lewis, *God in the Dock: Essays on Theology and Ethics*, ed. Walter Hooper (Grand Rapids, Mich.: Wm. B. Eerdmans Publishing Co., 1970), p. 66.

9. Lewis, *Problem of Pain*, chap. 5, pp. 77, 79.

10. Christensen, *C. S. Lewis on Scripture*, p. 65.

11. Lewis, *God in the Dock*, p. 66.

12. Christensen, *C. S. Lewis on Scripture*, pp. 92–93.

13. Lewis, *Letters to Malcolm*, letter 4.

14. Ibid., letter 5, p. 27.

15. Ibid., letter 10, pp. 55–56.

16. Ibid., letter 12, p. 65.

17. Ibid., letter 13, pp. 68–69.

18. Ibid., letter 13, p. 70.

19. Ibid., letter 18, pp. 98–99.

20. Ibid., p. 97.

21. Ibid., letter 19.

22. Ibid., letter 22, p. 124.

CHAPTER 8   Ethics

1. Chad Walsh, *C. S. Lewis: Apostle to the Skeptics* (New York: The Macmillan Company, 1949), p. 160.

2. Gilbert Meilaender, *The Taste for the Other: The Social and Ethical*

Thought of C. S. Lewis (Grand Rapids, Mich.: Wm. B. Eerdmans Publishing Co., 1978), pp. 1–2.

3. Lewis, *Mere Christianity*, bk. 2, chap. 1, p. 17.

4. C. S. Lewis, *The Abolition of Man, or Reflections on Education with Special Reference to the Teaching of English in the Upper Forms of Schools* (1943; reprint, New York: Macmillan Publishing Co., Inc., Macmillan Paperback Edition, 1965), pp. 27–29. The best part of this book is the appendix, in which Lewis cites examples of the Law from ancient civilizations, Norse and Icelandic sources, Stoic as well as Jewish and Christian writers.

5. Ibid., p. 34.

6. Lewis, *Mere Christianity*, bk. 1, chap. 4, p. 33.

7. Meilaender, *The Taste for the Other*, chap. 5.

8. Lewis, *That Hideous Strength*, chap. 14.

9. Lewis, *Out of the Silent Planet*, chap. 20, pp. 138–139.

10. Lewis, *Mere Christianity*, bk. 3, chap. 1, p. 71.

11. C. S. Lewis, *The Discarded Image: An Introduction to Medieval and Renaissance Literature* (Cambridge: Cambridge University Press, 1964), p. 114. Gilbert Meilaender compares this to the similar doctrine in Anders Nygren's *Agape and Eros*. Cf. *The Taste for the Other*, p. 55.

12. Lewis, *Four Loves*, chap. 6, pp. 178–180.

13. Lewis, *Screwtape Letters*, letter 18, pp. 81–82.

14. Meilaender, *The Taste for the Other*, pp. 64–70.

15. Lewis, *Mere Christianity*, bk. 3, chap. 3, p. 79.

16. White, *Image of Man*, chap. 8, pp. 175–176.

17. Lewis, *Mere Christianity*, bk. 3, chap. 5, pp. 89–90.

18. Lewis, *God in the Dock*, pp. 317–322.

19. W. H. Lewis, *Letters of C. S. Lewis*, p. 242.

20. Lewis, *Surprised by Joy*, chap. 6.

21. W. H. White, *Letters of C. S. Lewis*, p. 281.

22. Ibid., p. 292.

23. Lewis, *Four Loves*, chap. 4.

24. Lewis, *Mere Christianity*, bk. 3, chap. 7, p. 107.

25. C. S. Lewis, *The Weight of Glory and Other Addresses*, rev. ed. (New York: Macmillan Publishing Co., Inc., 1980), p. 53.

26. Lewis, *Screwtape Letters*, letter 5, pp. 25–26.

CHAPTER 9   The Last Things

1. Lewis, *Miracles*, chap. 14, pp. 126–128.

2. Lewis, *Reflections on the Psalms*, chap. 2, p. 9.

3. Lewis, *Letters to Malcolm*, letter 20, pp. 108–109.

4. Ibid., p. 109.

5. C. S. Lewis, *The World's Last Night and Other Essays* (New York: Harcourt, Brace and Company, 1960), pp. 105–106.

6. Lewis, *Problem of Pain*, chap. 8, p. 128.

7. Lewis, *Screwtape Letters*, letter 5, p. 25.

8. Ibid., letter 12, p. 56.

9. Ibid.

10. Ibid., letter 22, p. 103.

11. C. S. Lewis, *The Great Divorce* (New York: The Macmillan Company, 1946), p. 126.

12. Lewis, *Problem of Pain*, chap. 10, pp. 144–145.

13. Ibid., p. 146.

14. Ibid., p. 148.

15. Ibid., p. 150.

16. Ibid., p. 153. A musical expression of the cosmic dance might be the finale of the Beethoven C# minor quartet, op. 131.

17. Ibid.

18. Lewis, *Last Battle*, chap. 16, p. 184.

19. Lewis, *Screwtape Letters*, letter 31, pp. 147–148.

Chronological Listing of Lewis's Major Works

1967 *Christian Reflections*

1967 *Letters to an American Lady*

1967 *Spenser's Images of Life*

1970 *God in the Dock*

1977 *The Dark Tower and Other Stories*

1979 *They Stand Together*

Bibliography

BIBLIOGRAPHICAL ESSAY

The Bodleian Library at Oxford University in England and the Marion E. Wade Collection at Wheaton College, Wheaton, Illinois are the two major sources for the works of C. S. Lewis. The Wade Collection was begun in 1965 with a small number of books and fifteen letters of Lewis; its curator Clyde S. Kilby has made the collection second to none. It has over a thousand of Lewis's original letters and copies of several hundred others, most of them unpublished. It holds the Boxen manuscripts—stories written and illustrated by Lewis in his boyhood—and it also possesses photostat copies of the original material in the Bodleian. The Wade Collection is a superb achievement and is virtually complete, including a number of personal memorabilia of Lewis, as well as the celebrated wardrobe of the Narnian Chronicles. It is a delightful place in which to do research.

Although its cut-off date is June 1972, *C. S. Lewis: An Annotated Checklist* by Joe R. Christopher and Joan K. Ostling (Kent State University Press, 1974) is an indispensable source. The list divides the Lewis material into (1) General and Unclassifiable Items, including Special Periodicals, (2) Biographical Essays, Personality Sketches, and News Items, (3) Fiction and Poetry, (4) Religion and Ethics, (5) Literary Criticism, (6) Selected Book Reviews, and (7) Indices.

In 1965 Walter Hooper, the executor of the Lewis estate, printed a bibliography of primary sources upon which the preceding work is based. Father Hooper was Lewis's secretary at the time of the latter's death. He is a most important source for "Lewisiana," along with Prof. Clyde S. Kilby and Prof. Chad Walsh, whose *C. S. Lewis: Apostle to the Skeptics* first drew attention in 1949 to the Oxford don, at least in the United States.

Secondary and interpretative sources are too numerous to mention. I found particularly helpful Michael J. Christensen's *C. S. Lewis on Scripture*, William Luther White's *The Image of Man in C. S. Lewis* (for Lewis's anthropology), Clyde S. Kilby's *The Christian World of C. S. Lewis*, Paul Holmer's *C. S. Lewis The Shape of His Faith and Thought*, Humphrey Carpenter's *The Inklings*, James T. Como's *C. S. Lewis at the Breakfast Table*, Gilbert Meilaender's *The Taste for the Other* and the monthly bulletins of the New York C. S. Lewis Society issued by the secretary of the society, Mrs. John Kirkpatrick, New Haven, Conn. Mr. Gene McGovern, a personal friend of Walter Hooper's, was also an invaluable aid.

SELECTED BIBLIOGRAPHY

Carpenter, Humphrey. *The Inklings.* London: Allen & Unwin, 1978.

Christensen, Michael J. *C. S. Lewis on Scripture.* Waco, Tex.: Word Bks., 1979.

Christopher, Joe R., and Ostling, Joan K. *C. S. Lewis: An Annotated Checklist of Writings About Him and His Works.* Kent, Ohio: Kent State University Press, 1974.

Como, James T., ed. *C. S. Lewis at the Breakfast Table: And Other Reminiscences.* New York: Macmillan, 1979.

Cunningham, Richard B. *C. S. Lewis: Defender of the Faith.* Philadelphia: Westminster, 1967.

Derrick, Christopher. *C. S. Lewis and the Church of Rome.* San Francisco: Ignatius Press, 1981.

Gibb, Joselyn, ed. *Light on C. S. Lewis.* (Essays by Owen Barfield, Austin Farrar, J. A. W. Bennett, Nevill Coghill, John Lawlor, Stella Gibbons, Kathleen Raine, Chad Walsh, and Walter Hooper.) 1965. New York: Harcourt Brace Jovanovich, 1974; paperback, 1976.

Gibson, Evan. *C. S. Lewis, Spinner of Tales.* Grand Rapids, Mich.: Eerdmans, 1980.

Green, Roger Lancelyn, and Hooper, Walter. *C. S. Lewis: A Biography.* New York: Harcourt Brace Jovanovich, 1974; paperback, 1976.

Holmer, Paul L. *C. S. Lewis: The Shape of His Faith and Thought.* New York: Harper & Row, 1976.

Hooper, Walter. *Past Watchful Dragons: The Narnian Chronicles of C. S. Lewis.* New York: Macmillan, Collier Books, 1979.

Kilby, Clyde C. *The Christian World of C. S. Lewis.* Grand Rapids, Mich.: Eerdmans, 1964.

———. *Images of Salvation in the Fiction of C. S. Lewis.* Wheaton, Ill.: Harold Shaw, 1978.

Kranz, Gisbert. *C. S. Lewis: Studien zu Leben und Werk.* Bonn: Herbert Grundmann, 1974.

Kreeft, Peter. *C. S. Lewis: A Critical Essay*. Grand Rapids, Mich.: Eerdmans, 1969.

Meilaender, Gilbert. *The Taste for the Other: The Social and Ethical Thought of C. S. Lewis*. Grand Rapids, Mich.: Eerdmans, 1978.

Purtill, Richard L. *C. S. Lewis's Case for the Christian Faith*. New York: Harper & Row, 1981.

Sammons, Martha C. *A Guide through Narnia*. Wheaton, Ill.: Harold Shaw, 1979.

Schakel, Peter Jr., ed. *The Longing for a Form: Essays on the Fiction of C. S. Lewis*. Kent, Ohio: Kent State University Press, 1977.

Vanauken, Sheldon. *A Severe Mercy*. New York: Harper & Row, 1977.

Walsh, Chad. *C. S. Lewis: Apostle to the Skeptics*. New York: Macmillan, 1949; Folcraft, Pa.: Folcraft Library Editions, 1974.

————. *The Literary Legacy of C. S. Lewis*. New York: Harcourt Brace Jovanovich, 1979.

White, William Luther. *The Image of Man in C. S. Lewis*. Nashville: Abingdon, 1969.

Index